A Short Dictionary
of the New Testament

A Short Dictionary of the New Testament

Albert Rouet

Paulist Press
New York/Ramsey

Interior artwork and charts by Frank Sabatté, C.S.P.

Originally published under the title *Des Hommes Et Des Choses Du Nouveau Testament,* © 1979 Desclée De Brouwer. English translation © 1982 by The Missionary Society of St. Paul the Apostle in the State of New York.

Library of Congress
Catalog Card Number: 81-82435

ISBN: 0-8091-2400-9

Published by Paulist Press
545 Island Road, Ramsey, N.J. 07446

Printed and bound in the
United States of America

Contents

Introduction

We do not usually read a dictionary straight through, but this is not a dictionary to be used merely to look up the meaning of a word. It tries to make the human reality of the scenes in which Jesus lived come to life again. It wants to help the reader of the New Testament rediscover the environment which shaped the lives of the people of that time.

Yet we no longer live in that culture. We find certain actions very strange. For example the sower in Matthew 13:3–9 seems very inept. He throws his seed all over the place. We know that before our farmers sow they plow, but in Matthew's time seed was sown before plowing, simply because the blades of the plow were not strong enough to make a furrow and just covered up the grain thrown on the earth.

Our sower, then, does not actually know where he is sowing, because, having not yet turned the earth, he does not know whether it hides thorny roots or stones, or whether the neighbors will continue to walk across his field. He sowed because it was the right season, because there was land there. Later the true nature of the soil would be known. What are we to conclude? That this tells us nothing about the meaning of the parable? Not at all. Far from drawing from the text a voluntarist teaching about the good earth we must become if we are to be able to sow the word, the parable emphasizes that we must sow wherever we find earth, that all land calls out for grain, for an act of hope. Sow, sow, and sow more and the grain will spring up (cf. Mk. 4:26–29 and Jn. 4:37).

In addition, the attention to human realities allows us to understand even today the profoundly human interplay, the essential conflict involved both in the present and in the past. Here are three examples in rising order of importance.

1. The story of the paralytic. Mark speaks accurately of the earth "terrace" through which a hole was made (2:4). Luke transposed the story to a country where the houses were roofed with "tiles" (5:19). Similarly, Paul used comparisons drawn from an urban setting (sports, armies, architecture), and when he ventures to speak of grafting, his method would produce a magnificent wild tree, for he grafts backward (Rom. 11:17). What then does the transfer of the Gospel outside its initial cultural context mean for us?

1

2. The poor Samaritan woman. Why is verse 17 in John 4 interpreted as if she were leading the life of a trollop? Apparently she had already been repudiated four times. She is thus a rejected woman, cast aside, and she it is to whom Jesus speaks. Moreover, the status of women in Israel forbade a Jewish woman (the wife of Jairus, Mt. 9) from going to seek Jesus. She had to be a Phoenician to dare to approach him directly (Mt. 15) unless, of course, she had been introduced, as was true of the mother of James and John (Mt. 20).

3. Let us pause a moment on the third example, the text of Matthew 19 on marriage. It takes on its real dimensions if it is placed in the context of the social situation of the time, that is, if we take the time to observe the conflicts of power.

a. It is a question of repudiating a woman. Polygamy existed among the affluent (with the woman as a means of an alliance and an extension of power) and among the least respected classes (the woman as an outlet for misery). Between these two extremes stood the Pharisees. They wanted a holy, upright country, faithful to the Lord. It was a notable ambition but one which did not question the superiority of men over women or the inferior status of the latter. The difference between the sexes represented the first conflict of power. It is with that understanding that they ask Jesus their question.

b. The motive for repudiation is in question. Of the two schools of thought among the Pharisees, one took a broader view which tolerated repudiation for superficial reasons (the woman no longer gave pleasure). The other, stricter school required a serious reason (infidelity, sterility). The practice of repudiation was not itself a subject of debate. The snare was to force Jesus to take one of the alternative positions; if he appeared like any other rabbi, he would be judged insignificant. Jesus referred his inquisitors back to the act of God the Creator—before the law.

c. The argument turned to juridical forms: a certificate must be delivered. But then what power does this law serve? Jesus draws away from the problematic and goes back to the creation of man and woman.

d. While repudiation is no longer the subject (it has gotten lost), the question of power remains, one which commentators often neglect because they stop the paragraph on marriage at verse 9 and attach the following verses to the proposal for consecrated celibacy. The question of power still remains open, however, and linked to the question of marriage. The disciples are really afraid of losing their power ("If such is the case of a man"). Jesus then resumes this language. (He is actually talking on the same subject, that is, the man-woman relation.) But after having dealt with the indissolubility of marriage, he again takes up the social question of the form of power which has been exercised in marriage and which makes repudiation possible. He takes as his point of comparison those who in fact have no power: eunuchs. By throwing at the apostles the idea that marriage cannot be the place to express conflicts of power or of the domination of one over the other, he makes it a sign of obvious social significance.

From these examples could we work out a format for our reading? The subjects are too diverse for that, but we can at least ask these questions when reading any text of the New Testament.

1. To determine the place and the importance of the place, ask: Is it in the country, in the city, in Jerusalem? (The difference between the capital and the country was great.) Is the temple involved? Are there journeys and how are they being made?

2. In the case of an object, ask: Who made it? Who transported it or sold it? Is its cost known? Is it a sign of poverty? Who ordinarily uses it? Does it have a religious significance (like a rabbi's robe)? Has it any relation to the temple? Is it considered pure or impure?

3. If it is a person, ask: What is his status in life? What are his alliances? What power does he have? What is his religious position because of his knowledge and training? because of his political connections? What is his position vis-à-vis the temple, the law, the Pharisees, the Romans? Is his occupation pure or impure? vile or noble? How does he work? (Peter, in John 21, worked naked. He dressed to go into the water— and he did not know how to swim.) With whom is he in business? What are their financial and political interests?

4. Do these data describe agricultural, urban, or commercial surroundings? How do these social relations influence religious attitudes, and are they influenced by religion?

5. Lastly, what change does Jesus introduce? How does this change, or partial change, come about? What are the favorable reactions? What interests oppose the change? What are the elements in the situation which Jesus does not change?

Chapter 1

Agriculture, Fishing and Commerce

Palestine was an agricultural country. The cultivated land was found chiefly in the center, in Samaria, and the north, Galilee. The south, Judea, was used more for raising livestock.

Principal Crops

Wheat, both hard and soft, and barley were planted. Sown in November and December, wheat was harvested around May and June. In Galilee and Samaria, where the holdings were large, a high yield was obtained.

Each family had a garden for its own needs but a great part of the agricultural production was exported to Rome.

In addition, Palestine produced olives, which were both consumed in the country and used to make oil. It had more olive trees then than now. The Jericho region also produced dates. Wine was produced in good quantity but not drunk every day. It was cut with a little water as the alcohol content was high. Some wines were like the French aperitifs. Wine was allowed to age up to seven years.

Palestine also produced aromatic plants, that is, plants with a fragrant odor, which served as bases for perfumes used to embalm the dead. Balm, a kind of resin, was much in demand. Palestine also brought in incense for use in the temple where, in a single year, the morning and evening sacrifices required 265 pounds.

Finally, wheat was sold to pay taxes in kind. At the time of Christ, wheat was three times more valuable than barley.

Beginnings of agriculture:		
B.C. 6000	Galilee and Iran	Two kinds of wild wheat and barleys
5000	Galilee and Iran	Ordinary wheat
3000	Galilee and Iran	Rye
	Egypt	Lentils
	Palestine	Olives
	Egypt	Dates
	Iran	Figs
2000	Palestine	Oats
		Chick peas

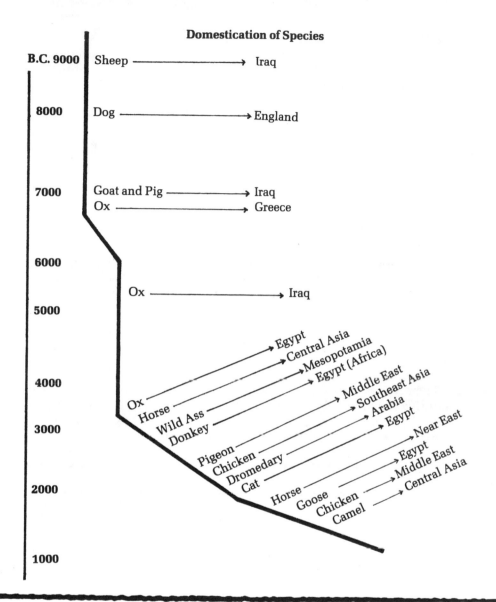

Domestication of Species

B.C. 9000	Sheep ————————→	Iraq
8000	Dog ————————→	England
7000	Goat and Pig ————————→	Iraq
	Ox ————————→	Greece
6000		
5000	Ox ————————→	Iraq
4000	Ox ————————→	Egypt
	Horse ————————→	Central Asia
	Wild Ass ————————→	Mesopotamia
	Donkey ————————→	Egypt (Africa)
3000	Pigeon ————————→	Middle East
	Chicken ————————→	Southeast Asia
	Dromedary ————————→	Arabia
	Cat ————————→	Egypt
2000	Horse ————————→	Near East
	Goose ————————→	Egypt
	Chicken ————————→	Middle East
	Camel ————————→	Central Asia
1000		

Catastrophes in Palestine:

B.C. 66	Drought
64	Hurricane during harvest
37	Siege of Jerusalem by Herod; famine
31	Earthquake
29	Plague
25	Drought; famine
A.D. 47	Famine under Emperor Claudius
65	Water failure

Recipe for purifying oil:

1. Pour the oil extracted from the crushed olives into a pot of very hot, salted water.
2. Stir well with a stick. Let stand.
3. Impurities will fall to the bottom; the pure oil will float on top of the water.

Husbandry

Small livestock (goats, sheep) were raised. Cows were raised where there was water, as in Galilee and on the coastal plain. In the south there were herds of dromedaries. Rich men had a horse and donkeys were often used.

Palestine exported little meat; it produced just enough for itself. A large number of animals were sacrificed at the temple.

In the north, swine were raised, but only by non-Jews, for Jews did not eat this meat.

Fishing

Fish, especially dried fish, often constituted the mainstay of the daily meal. Fishermen, considered to have an honorable status, were numerous around the Sea of Galilee and on the shores of the Mediterranean, but here they were not all Jews. On the Sea of Galilee, the fishing was done in boats with teams of six to eight men, each with a team leader and teams sometimes banded together. A large net was used, the seine, which was 1,650 feet long by 10 feet wide. Fishing was also done by line or with a sweep net, thrown by a single man. The sea contained pike, carp, and perch. Jews would not eat fish without scales, such as eels.

Mines

There were almost no mines, aside from the numerous quarries of building stone. Herod was permitted by the Emperor Augustus to exploit the copper mines at Cyprus but a heavy customs tax was imposed on metal products. Bitumen was extracted around the Dead Sea.

Commerce

Trade routes followed the coast (Gaza, Ptolemais, Caesarea) or converged on Jerusalem, where pilgrimages formed an important basis for trade. Herod had attracted Greek colonists with a good sense for business to the new or improved cities, and Jews established shops there, and even banks (Mt. 25:27; Lk. 19:23).

A poor country, ravaged by numerous disasters, Palestine lived mostly on its own resources. It imported non-agricultural products, and only Galilee exported wheat. In Galilee, the products of the large estates, which had slaves, often went to the cities of Tyre and Sidon, where their masters lived. The Roman taxes were heavy. The situation of the so-called "people of the land," i.e., the poorer class (who were considered inferior also in religious knowledge), was such that they were barely able to survive.

Recipe for making aromatic ointments:

1. *Gather fragrant plants (laurel, myrrh, thyme). Put the leaves in oil.*

2. *For color, add sorrel (green) or cinnabar (orange). Add pleasant smelling resins (balms) such as sandalwood from India or cypress shavings, according to the desired fragrance. Crush thoroughly.*

3. *Wash in tepid water, dry, and gather together carefully, taking out twigs, etc.*

4. *Boil one day in water, add perfumes, and let stand overnight.*

5. *Reheat slowly; add oil and mix well. Let stand several days.*

6. *Boil and filter.*

(This recipe dates from the time of Christ)

Chapter 2

Canaanites

Origin of the Word

"Canaanite," from the word "Canaan," is a very broad term, designating all of the traditional, non-Jewish inhabitants of Palestine. The word "Canaan" comes originally from the Mesopotamian language and means "red" because of the reddish purple dye produced in the country. Translated into Greek, this word became "Phoenician"—"purple" or "crimson."

History of Canaan

Settled very early, this region became a passageway between Africa and Asia, and there was a constant influx of peoples. The main invasions came from the north and east, but others were by sea. The principal settlers were:

1. A very ancient pre-historic people who grouped in small communities at Jericho one hundred centuries before Christ.

2. In the third and fourth millennia a push of people arrived from the east who were fleeing the great Assyrian empires, and Semitic tribes came up from Arabia.

3. During the nineteenth and eighteenth centuries before Jesus Christ, other Semitic people migrated, nomads coming from Mesopotamia. Abraham's clan was part of this movement.

4. In the seventeenth and sixteenth centuries B.C., Indo-Germanic tribes came down from the steppes of central Asia, from as far as India, Persia and Germany. The "Hyksos" also arrived, driven before them.

5. In the fourteenth century B.C. Hittites infiltrated from the north (present-day Turkey).

6. In the thirteenth century B.C. peoples from present-day Lebanon (Tyre and Sidon) reached Galilee, then moved into the center of Palestine. They formed the basic group of the Canaanite people.

7. In the twelfth century B.C. the "People of the Sea," from the area of the Aegean Sea and Crete, invaded. Stopped by Pharaoh Rameses III, one segment of these people settled down. They were the Philistines and from their name comes the word "Palestine." They destroyed the equilibrium between Canaanites and Israelites, and the latter, in resistance, regrouped into a kingdom (cf. Saul, David). The Philistines established themselves on the coast.

8. Then came the conquests: by the Babylonians, 800–600 B.C., the Greeks in the fourth century B.C., and the Romans in the first century B.C., each leaving its traces.

Because the land of Palestine was a passageway for caravans, other foreigners also settled there. Nomads came there to live, and even former pirates who settled on the coast. Among them:

1. Arabs entered from the east and south.
2. Merchants from Nabataea, a country to the south of the Dead Sea, settled in the south, near the Petra-Gaza road.
3. Greeks came to trade such items as felt, footwear, and pottery. Judea received them badly but Herod welcomed them.
4. Merchants from Damascus or other cities came and stayed.

Therefore Palestine was not a country with a uniform population. Actually, Canaanite designates the basic, non-Jewish population of Palestine, those who had lived there for a very long time and were neither Greek nor Roman. The source of this population was the same as in Tyre and Sidon, present-day Lebanon.

In the Bible, which tried to establish connections among peoples, the Canaanites were said to come from Ham, the son of Noah who had made fun of his father (Gen. 9:18–27). This was not a question of physical descent, but an attempt to describe the relations between the inhabitants and to insure the primacy of the people of the covenant.

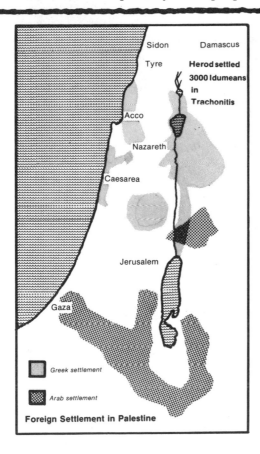

Foreign Settlement in Palestine

Chapter 3

Childhood

At the time of Christ, children were not thought of in the same way as today. They were closely dependent on their family and raised among adults. There were few schools, except when a scribe gathered some boys around himself. The child was an entity among adults.

Children were born at home. Because of the lack of hygiene there was much sickness, and the infant mortality rate was high. A midwife came to help the mother. (The midwife was the only person who could exercise a profession on the sabbath.) If the birth was difficult, the family had recourse to almost magical practices, especially the ordinary people; for example, a piece of parchment with a passage from the Law would be placed on the mother.

The mother was surrounded by women friends. As soon as the child was born, the father took it on his knee to show that he accepted it, and the child was wrapped in swaddling clothes.

Eight days later, a boy was circumcised at home or in the synagogue. The father gave him a name. The child was called X, son of X, as, for example, Simon, son of John. The names given might be Aramaic, which became the language of Palestine when Hebrew was no longer used, such as Bartholomew (Bar means "son of") or Martha, or they could be Greek, such as Philip, Andrew, or Stephen, or Latin, such as Rufus or Niger.

If a woman conceives and bears a male child, then she shall be considered unclean seven days. . . . And on the eighth day the flesh of the foreskin shall be circumcised. Then she shall continue thirty-three days in the blood of her purifying; she shall not touch any hallowed thing nor come into the sanctuary. . . . But if she bears a female child, then she shall be unclean two weeks . . . and she shall continue in the blood of her purifying sixty-six days. And when the days of her purifying are completed, whether for a son or for a daughter, she shall bring to the priest the animals for a sacrifice.
Lev. 12:2–7

Since childbirth involved a loss of blood, a mother was "impure" for forty days after the birth of a boy and for eighty days after the birth of a girl; in other words, her condition was considered alien to the holiness of religion. (See the chapter on Ritual Purity.)

Forty days later, the father offered a sacrifice. If the child was the first-born son, he belonged by custom to God and the sacrifice took the place of offering the child.

An infant was nursed for a long time—about twenty months. A father was required to pay for a child's needs until he was six. He could not sell him into slavery, although apparently twelve-year-old children may have been slaves.

What games did the children play? They had dolls and earthen or wood animals, played blind man's bluff, hopscotch, and dice, and skipped rope. In the country a child helped with work in the fields very early and often watched the little family flock. In the town he frequently learned a trade from his father or from a friend in the same profession.

The father watched over his sons carefully, his strictness even going to the point of corporal punishment. The mother educated the daughters at home.

At his thirteenth year, the age when Moses was said to have left the daughter of Pharaoh, the boy reached his majority. Subject to the law, he accompanied his father to the temple, going into the men's court, as Jesus did (Lk. 2:41–51).

The average life-span was thirty-five years.

While completely accepted, the child was nevertheless thought of only in relation to adults. In taking children as models, Jesus reversed

Consecrate to me all the first-born;
whatever is the first to open the
womb among the people of Israel,
both of men and of beasts, is mine.
Every first-born of man among
your sons, you shall redeem.
Ex. 13:2, 13

And they were bringing children
to him, that he might touch them;
and the disciples rebuked them. But
when Jesus saw it he was indignant,
and said to them, "Let the children
come to me. Do not hinder them, for
to such belongs the kingdom of God.
Truly, I say to you, whoever does not
receive the kingdom of God like a
child shall not enter it." And he took
them in his arms and blessed them,
laying his hands upon them.
Mk. 10:13–16

this perspective, not in the sense that one was to remain childish but to regain the filial spirit and a sense of trust.

Circumcision

For hygienic reasons, many African and Asian peoples cut the foreskin of boys, that is, the skin at the end of the penis. The Israelites seem to have taken circumcision from the Egyptians, although many Semitic peoples already practiced it.

Originally done at the end of childhood with a flint knife (Jos. 5:2), a sign of how old the practice was, circumcision served as a rite of passage to adulthood. Later on it began to be performed earlier and earlier. At the time of Christ, circumcision was performed eight days after birth; either the father did it while giving the child his name, or it was done by an elder in the synagogue, and it could even be performed on the sabbath. At that time, its meaning was to show, by a permanent mark, that one belonged to the people of God. By contrast, pagans were considered the "uncircumcised."

To show the value of circumcision, the Bible traces this rite back to Abraham, "father of the chosen people."

Sayings of rabbis: "Great is circumcision."

Rabbi Ismael said: Great is circumcision because it was on this basis that thirteen covenants were concluded.

Rabbi Jose said: Great is circumcision because it allows the sabbath to be violated. (Circumcision was permitted on the sabbath.)

Rabbi Jesus: Great is circumcision because it was not delayed even an hour for Moses the Just.

Rabbi Nehemia: Great is circumcision because it suspends the interdict against wounding on the sabbath.

Another rabbi: Great is circumcision because even after our father Abraham had fulfilled all the commandments, he was not called perfect until he had been circumcised.

And again: Great is circumcision because, if it did not exist, the Holy One (God) would not have created his world, as Jeremiah says: "Thus says Yahweh: If my covenant had not existed day and night I would not have established the laws of heaven and earth." (Jer. 33:25).

Chapter 4

Communications

From the time of David, two north-south routes crossed Palestine, one along the coast running north from Egypt and one in the center going up from Beersheba to Jerusalem, Bethel and Galilee. In Galilee this road divided: toward Damascus or toward the Phoenician ports. In the south, the caravan routes converged on Jericho and Jerusalem, and on Gaza. East of the Jordan a road followed the river, but higher up the valley it was impracticable because of brush and flooding.

The roads were made of earth, but paved in places with stones. The Roman conquest introduced carefully paved roads. Rome placed great importance on its network of roads as a means of insuring the permanence of its conquests, and the legions constructed and maintained the public roads built at the cost of the state. Villages were also connected by a large number of local roads maintained by the towns and the large landholders whose estates they crossed. Lastly, there were private roads on large properties.

The Sanhedrin did very little for the highways, except the one toward Mesopotamia because a high priest appointed by Herod had come from there.

The Romans introduced their techniques of construction into Palestine. They linked the capitals (Jerusalem, Sebaste, Sepphoris, Caesarea) so that they could move rapidly into any place.

A Roman road was from twenty to twenty-seven feet wide. Markers with the name of the emperor during whose reign the road was constructed indicated the distances to the principal places in the region. The coastal road was completed by Nero.

The central axis, built along the crest to escape ambushes, ran through Samaria. From Jerusalem, two roads led to Gaza, two to the sea, one to Jericho and beyond it to the Jordan. The "king's highway" linked Caesarea with Scythopolis and the East.

pavement of cut stone

ditch 1.6m

earth • sand

sand and small stones

.base of large stones

A stage was about twenty-eight miles, and there was a toll. There was also an inn for travelers every twenty-eight miles. Horseshoes, bridles and horse collars were unknown. To draw more than eleven hundred pounds would risk fouling the harness.

Since robbery was rampant around Jerusalem, people traveled in groups, much of the time on foot or often on donkeys. Caravans of camels filed across the country, some even going as far as China for silk.

The imperial post operated regularly for the needs of the empire. With relays every seven and a half miles, a courier covered forty-seven miles daily. The post relays had fresh horses, stables, and sheds and sometimes a small camp for protection. To give an idea of travel time, it took ten days to go from Egypt to Caesarea.

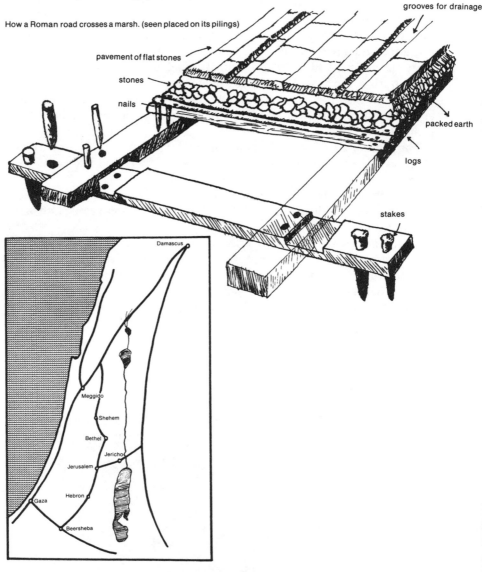

How a Roman road crosses a marsh. (seen placed on its pilings)

grooves for drainage

pavement of flat stones

stones

nails

packed earth

logs

stakes

Damascus

Meggido

Shehem

Bethel

Jericho

Jerusalem

Hebron

Gaza

Beersheba

Navigation

Palestine had no navigable waterways. The five hundred-ton barges used on the Nile to transport blocks of stone were never seen there. After Tyre and Sidon, the ports were Caesarea, Ptolemais, and Joppa. The Egyptian, Tyrian or Roman boats were "flatirons with sails." The average ship was not larger than one hundred and thirty-five feet by thirty-three feet. It could carry from three hundred to three hundred and fifty tons. The Egyptian ships were more delicate. Heavier ships were built, but because they had no rudder, they could not easily be steered.

Navigation stopped during the winter, except for coastal vessels.

Types of Ships

Vessels with oars, of the galley type, which had up to one hundred and seventy rowers.

Warships and pleasure ships.

For trade, the Romans used the *oneraria* for grain, wine, oil; the *corbeta*, equivalent to the corvette, with a rounded front and well designed, which carried one hundred and thirty men and a crew of forty; the *ponto*, a heavy grain ship.

The Phoenicians had cargo ships that were faster because of their big sails.

Trading ships, especially Greek ones, used both sail and oars.

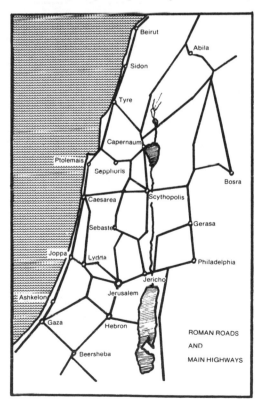

ROMAN ROADS
AND
MAIN HIGHWAYS

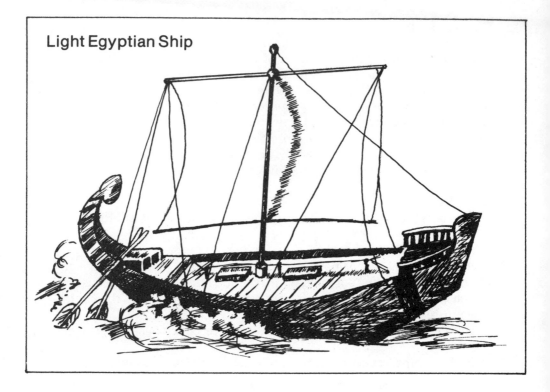

Light Egyptian Ship

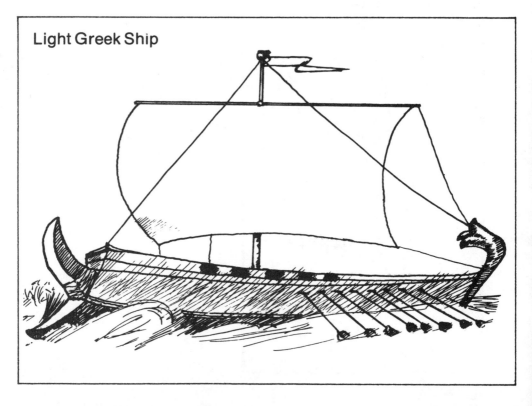

Light Greek Ship

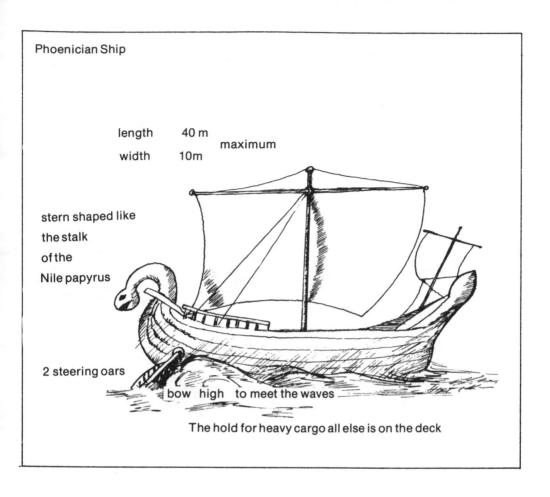

Phoenician Ship

length   40 m
                    maximum
width   10m

stern shaped like
the stalk
of the
Nile papyrus

2 steering oars

bow   high   to meet the waves

The hold for heavy cargo all else is on the deck

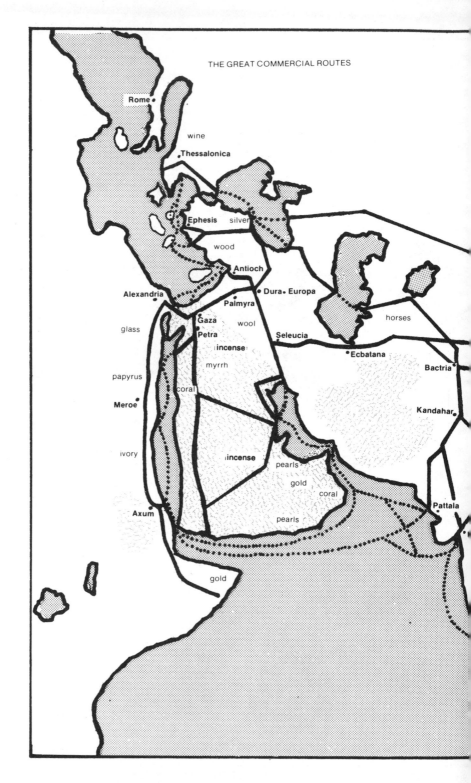

THE GREAT COMMERCIAL ROUTES

Rome •

wine

• Thessalonica

Ephesis   silver

wood

• Antioch

Alexandria •   • Dura • Europa

Palmyra

Gaza   wool   horses

glass   Petra   Seleucia

incense   • Ecbatana

myrrh   Bactria •

papyrus   coral

Meroe •   Kandahar •

ivory   incense

pearls

gold

coral

Axum •   Pattala

pearls

gold

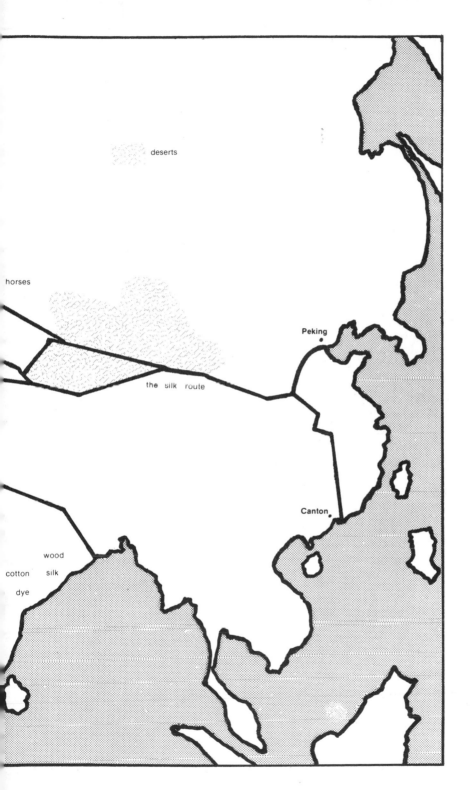

deserts

horses

Peking

the silk route

Canton

wood

cotton   silk

dye

Chapter 5

Essenes

Community of the Dead Sea Scrolls

The word "Essene," which is not in the Bible, seems to come from "hasim," the pious (men).

Among themselves, they used the terms the "elect," the "holy," the "poor ones," the "sons of light."

Knowledge about them was greatly increased by the discovery, in 1947, of manuscripts hidden in caves near the Dead Sea.

1. A Community in a State of War

In a desert near the Dead Sea, away from roads and towns and near springs of water and large cisterns, there lived a community of men and women who did not permit polygamy or divorce, and who had rejected the mode of worship of the temple at Jerusalem because it had failed to return to the old calendar and the ancient rites and it had changed the families from which the high priests came.

The baptist movement

At the time of Jesus, there were popular movements proclaiming salvation to all through immersion, i.e., baptism, in living water, even to sinners and pagans. Groups sprang up as far away as Mesopotamia and Iran. (Cf. John the Baptist and Acts 19:1–5.) They baptized to take away faults and to announce the nearness of the Messiah and they rejected the bloody sacrifices of the temple.

Today is the day set by God to overturn and cause the fall of the Prince of the Kingdom of Perdition. He will send his everlasting aid to the party which he has redeemed by the power of an angel whom he has made full of glory in order to rule over his Empire. The angel Michael in eternal light will bring to all Israel light in joy, peace and blessing to the party of God, to exalt among the gods the Empire of Michael and the domination of Israel over all flesh.

(Taken from "The War of the Son of Light against the Son of Darkness," 14.)

This community had a strict hierarchical order: at the top, priests, who had all the power; then, Levites; next, lay chiefs and members. Obedience was an absolute condition of membership in the group. There were about four thousand Essenes living in several communities. Many were celibate. One group existed in Egypt, the "therapeutists," i.e. "healers"; another lived near Damascus.

The head, also called the "superintendent," was between thirty and fifty years of age and was the father of the community. He was told of faults committed, received candidates and instructed new members. He expelled those who did not follow the rules. Scribes explained the law.

The community anticipated a military liberation by a judge-Messiah. Once the community had been purified of pagans and bad Jews, this Messiah, the Son of David, would inaugurate a return to paradise. The people would then be governed by a second messiah, the most important "son of Aaron," that is, a high priest.

2. Pure and Hard

The community observed great fidelity to God, to the covenant and to the law of Moses, as well as to the priests and to the traditional families of priests. They kept the old calendar, refused compromise with the law and required of each member a ritual purity as great as that of the high priest—hence the numerous ablutions.

Candidates asked to enter. For two years they were "novices"—that is, they were progressively introduced into the community and obeyed the rule. Upon admission, a candidate donated his property to the group. Disobedient members were excluded for a time or for good.

Manual labor was highly valued. In the evening, Scripture was studied. Meals in common were very important.

Their doctrine divided the world into two groups: the good and the evil. The good lived forever and the evil died forever. Personal faults were purified by the ablutions of the baths and by fasting.

Places where Essene manuscripts were found

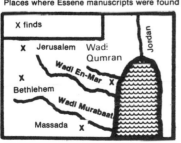

Since they were considered to be rigid, austere and steadfast, Herod did not require an oath of fidelity from them, for their rule forbade swearing.

3. *Connections with the Gospels*

The Essenes' texts, the Dead Sea Scrolls, contain copies of the books of the Old Testament, commentaries on the prophets, and the community's rules and prayers. We must not exaggerate the connections between the Gospels and the Qumran Essenes. The contacts are at the level of words ("son of light"), or through the attraction felt by their righteousness. But the Gospel rejects their hardness, their tendency to classify men and their view of the Messiah as a judge. Jesus proclaimed pardon and love.

Historical reference points:

167–142 B.C.: *Jewish struggles against the kings of Syria named Antiochus for their political and religious independence.*

After 100 B.C.: *A great man, the "Teacher of Righteousness," was exiled by the high priest of Jerusalem, leader of the people. He founded the Qumran community.*

June 21, 68 A.D.: *The Romans took Jericho and attacked Qumran. The manuscripts were hidden in the caves.*

Table of punishments:

Foolish laughter: forbidden the ablution baths for two months.

Gross word: forbidden the baths for three months.

Lying: forbidden the baths for six months and food reduced by a fourth.

Criticism: Baths forbidden for one year and food reduced.

Chapter 6

Feasts

The feasts celebrated God's intervention in history. They therefore celebrated the birth of the people by recreating the founding event. When a Jew offered the first fruits of his harvest at the temple, he said: "Today I declare to the Lord God that I have come into the land which the Lord swore to our fathers to give us" (Dt. 26:31). The people recognized the gratuitousness of God's choice; nothing predestined them to become God's people. The feast, in a sense, "constituted" the people.

Three great feasts set the rhythm of the year. These were "pilgrimage feasts," since going to the temple at Jerusalem was obligatory (Dt. 16).

Calendars

These present a complicated problem, since some followed the lunar cycle and some the solar, and the two coincided only every nineteen years.

1. Lunar calendar

This was the official calendar, known as the "Greek" calendar, which came from the nomads. Each month began with the new moon. It was worked out as follows:

Twelve months of twenty-nine and a half days each equaled three hundred and fifty-four days. An additional month of thirty days was added every three years or, beginning with the fourth century, seven months every nineteen years. This calendar was used in the temple. The year began with the first spring moon, a practice coming from Babylon. Previously the year had begun in the autumn.

2. Solar calendar

Twelve months of thirty days, equaling three hundred and sixty-four days or fifty-two weeks.

Feasts always fell on the same day of the week: Passover on Wednesday, Pentecost on Sunday.

This calendar was used at Qumran. With it, Christ's Last Supper would have taken place on Tuesday evening.

The beginning of the year

Varied according to the people.

In the Olympiads, it began July 1 from 776 B.C. to A.D.

In Rome, on January 1, from its foundation in 753 B.C. In 45 B.C. Julius Caesar invented the bisextile or leap year.

In the period of the Seleucids in Antioch, October 1, 312 B.C.

The date for the beginning of the Christian era was fixed in 526 by an Armenian monk, Dennis the Little, at March 25, 754 of the Roman era. He was in error by six years.

Today, for the Jews, July 1, 1982 began the year 5742.

A year was often computed from the accession of an emperor. The fifteenth year of Tiberias ran from April 19, 28 to April 18, 29.

1. Passover

This celebrated the new moon in the spring, on the 13th or 14th of Nisan, the first month of the Jewish year. It resulted when two feasts had been united under King Josiah (640–609):

a. The feast of nomad shepherds, who immolated a lamb in the spring. This feast is linked to the exodus (Ex. 12).

b. The feast of farmers, who offered first fruits: the new, unleavened bread.

Reserved for the circumcised, this week-long feast recalled the deliverance from Egypt, the creation and the exodus; it begged for the Messiah. During the Roman occupation, however, these themes had to be muted.

On the 13th of Nisan, in the evening, the householder searched his home to remove and burn every scrap of old bread. (He could take until the 15th of Nisan at noon to do this.)

In the afternoon of the 14th of Nisan, at the temple, every Israelite slaughtered a lamb or a kid. A priest took the blood and poured it at the foot of the altar. At nightfall, the Passover meal was eaten by families or by other groups of ten persons. They reclined on couches, because this had been considered the position of free men since the time of the Greek influence.

The meal proceeded in this fashion:

The first cup, for the blessing, was offered to the one presiding.

Unleavened bread, bitter herbs and sauces were offered.

A child asked: "In what way is this night different from other nights?"

The father, or whoever was presiding, would recite the story of the exodus in terms of a profession of faith.

The roasted lamb was eaten without the bones being broken, with the unleavened bread and the bitter herbs.

The second cup was drunk and the first section of the "Great Hallel" (Pss. 112–114) was recited.

The third cup, the cup of thanksgiving, was taken.

The second section of the "Great Hallel," Pss. 115–117, was sung.

The fourth cup and the blessing followed.

The day after the paschal sabbath, the first handful of barley was offered.

Samaritans celebrated the Passover on Mount Garizim, standing, as prescribed in Exodus 12.

2. Pentecost

This was called the Feast of Weeks, because it ended the fifty days or seven weeks of the paschal season. The first fruits of the grain harvest were then offered to God. It was considered the feast of the covenant by the second century A.D.; that is, it commemorated the gift of the law on

Sinai because the Jews had reached Sinai in the third month (after two lunar months).

3. Tents

Called the Feast of Booths or Tabernacles, this feast came at the end of the autumn harvest. The products of the soil, such as palm nuts and lemons, were offered to God, and it was customary to live for a week in booths made of leafy branches, some being shaped like a platform for the house. This was in memory of both the sojourn in the desert and the dedication of the temple of Solomon. The last day of the feast was the most solemn (Jn. 7:37).

Every morning priests went in procession to draw water from the fountain of Siloam; they then processed around the altar of holocausts singing Psalm 119, and finally poured the water on the altar.

In the evening, four huge gold candelabra were lighted in the Court of the Women. The light could be seen all over Jerusalem and assumed a messianic meaning: The Messiah is coming! Keep watch (Jn. 8:12).

4. Other Feasts

a. Yom Kippur was the feast of atonement for sin, "the fast." It took place five days before the Feast of Tents, with strict fasting and sacrifices for sin. The temple was purified by the sprinkling of blood. The high priest entered the Holy of Holies and placed his hands on the head of a scapegoat; then the animal, to whom the sins of the people had thus been transferred, was driven into the desert.

b. The Feast of the Dedication, in December, recalled the purifying of the temple by Judas Maccabeus in 164 B.C. (Jn. 10:22). A great fire was lighted and the flame was carried to Modin, the land of the Maccabees.

There were other secondary feasts, such as Purim or "Lots," a very joyful feast which recalled the story of Esther.

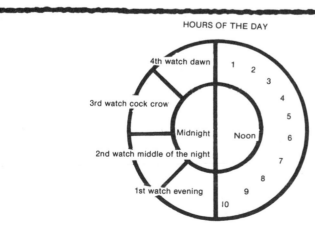

HOURS OF THE DAY

25

Chapter 7

Herod the Great

In order to understand the rise of Herod, it must be remembered that Palestine was affected by the turmoil of internal wars in Italy. Whatever happened in Rome reverberated in all countries of the Mediterranean world. Every prince tried to guess who was going to win in Rome.

1. "Mixed Blood"

Herod was not really a Jew. He had no right to be king and became one through an extraordinary combination of circumstances. All his life he held fast to this power to which he could lay no claim.

This is how it happened. In order to have peace in Italy and come to power, a Roman general, Pompey, wanted first to crush Rome's enemies in the East. He took Jerusalem in 63 B.C., bringing Jewish independence to an end. To govern the country, Pompey appointed a descendant of the Maccabeus family which had championed Jewish independence in the second century. This leader was also the high priest. He was subject to the Roman governor in Syria and paid tribute to Rome—a very heavy tribute. To watch over this Jewish leader, Pompey appointed an assistant, Antipater, an Idumean leader. (The Indumeans were a small, semi-Jewish tribe living in the south of Palestine, and Antipater had been helpful to the Romans.)

Antipater had two sons by the daughter of an Arab chief. The boys were named Phasael and Herod, and the latter was ten when Pompey took Jerusalem. Antipater's influence continued to grow.

2. Moving to Power

In 47 B.C. Caesar confirmed the high priest Hyrcanus II in his position, and as procurator of Judea he named Antipater, who had become a Roman citizen. He also made Phasael governor of Jerusalem and Herod governor of Galilee. Herod wiped out opponents and bandits and put down all revolts.

In 43 B.C. Antipater was poisoned, perhaps with the help of Hyrcanus. Herod allied himself with the high priest's family by marrying his granddaughter (one of the ten wives he was to have). To gain Herod's favor, Mark Antony, the Roman ruler of the Eastern empire, named him ruler of Galilee and Samaria, and he also appointed Phasael as ruler of Judea. The Jews resented this and revolted, but all opponents were killed.

In 40 B.C. the Parthians, a people hostile to Rome, invaded Palestine. They appointed Antigone, a nephew of Hyrcanus, as king of Judea, and Phasael, Herod's brother, died at their hands. Herod fled with his family to Masada, then to Alexandria and finally to Rome.

To protect itself against the Parthians, the Roman Senate, at the suggestion of Mark Antony and Octavius Caesar, named Herod king of Judea. As king, friend and ally of the Roman people, Herod then returned to Palestine. He fought Antigone (39–37 B.C.), and in the summer of 37 he took Jerusalem with the help of Roman legions. However, his protector Antony was defeated at Actium in 31 by Octavius. Herod hastened to meet the conqueror who, after becoming the Emperor Augustus, never failed to support Herod, and Herod, in turn, remained faithful to him.

3. *Herod as Sole King*

An astute diplomat, courageous soldier and fine administrator, Herod was a great success. While he was subject to Rome in matters of foreign policy, he did whatever he wished in his own country in regard to both the Romans and the Jews. He reigned like the kings in other countries, in the Greek style, with a large court and many foreign mercenaries. Greek was the official language of his court, and his annual revenue came to nine hundred talents.

His policy was grand. He restored broad frontiers to his kingdom as he rebuilt cities and founded new ones, populating them with foreigners. In religious matters, he was somewhat contemptuous of Jewish laws and went so far as to place a Roman eagle on the face of the temple. All oppo-

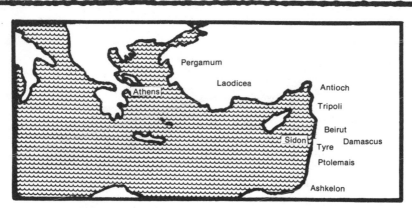

HEROD'S BUILDING PROJECTS OUTSIDE OF PALESTINE

"You may indeed set up a king over you whom the Lord your God will choose. One from among your brethren you shall set as king over you; you may not put a foreigner who is not your brethren over you" (Dt. 17:15).

This was a time of enormous problems in Italy, with social revolts and struggles among the ambitious. There was rivalry between two factions:

70–46: Pompey against Julius Caesar

43–29: Mark Antony against Octavius Caesar

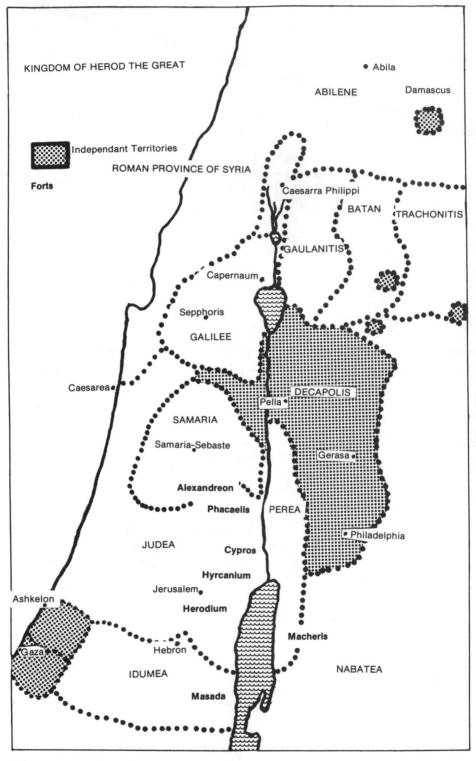

KINGDOM OF HEROD THE GREAT

• Abila

ABILENE   Damascus

Independant Territories

ROMAN PROVINCE OF SYRIA

Forts

Caesarra Philippi

BATAN   TRACHONITIS

GAULANITIS

Capernaum

Sepphoris

GALILEE

Caesarea•

DECAPOLIS

Pella•

SAMARIA

Samaria-Sebaste

Gerasa•

Alexandreon

Phacaelis   PEREA

JUDEA   **Cypros**

Hyrcanium

Jerusalem•

Ashkelon   **Herodium**

Gaza   **Macheris**

Hebron

NABATEA

IDUMEA

Masada

28

nents were killed. In Jerusalem he built a gymnasium, a palace, and a fortress, and, most important, he restored the temple. The work, begun on the temple in 19 B.C., allowed it to be reopened for worship very quickly, though it was not to be fully completed until 64 A.D.

Herod was hated by the Jews as a non-Jew, as the murderer of the old priestly family, and because of his ties to Rome and his lack of respect for Jewish customs. He died at Jericho in 4 B.C.

Herod and his sons' plots:
Herod was constantly at war with his family. In B.C.:
35 he killed his brother-in-law;
29 he killed one of his wives;
18 he killed a sister-in-law;
18–17 two of his sons raised in Rome revolted;
4 he killed his heir Antipater a few days before dying himself.

HEROD THE GREAT'S COURT

THE KING

1. Area of influence of family and friends

Intimates
"Cousins and friends" (so-called, not necessarily relatives). Rank first in honor; many Greeks. In addition:
One philosopher and court historian.
One teacher of eloquence.
One Roman officer to teach Aramaic.
One commander in chief.

Guests
received at the palace:
Sons-in-law of Emperor Augustus.
Envoys of neighboring kings.

Relatives
and relatives of wives, among them the minister of finances, keeper of the seals.

The Harem
One queen at head.
Nine to ten official wives.
Many concubines.
Children.
Servants (eunuchs).

OFFICIALS

2. Area of government

One secretary to the king (all correspondence).
One treasurer.
Three officers of the armies.
One bodyguard (king's companion, of Arab origin) who was an officer of the royal chamber.
Two high ranking guards from the Army Corps.

Tutors of royal princes and companions of princes (sons of nobles, raised with them).
Three officers of the chamber (eunuchs).
One cup bearer.
One majordomo.
One chamberlain. Had entree to the king's chamber; entrusted with most serious affairs of state.

3. Area of operation

Guards
Five hundred men plus foreign troops, e.g., four hundred Gauls, Cleopatra's former guards.

Others
Five hundred persons (a few eunuchs, many slaves, some freed).
Porters, master of the hunt and royal hunters; barbers, doctor, jewelers, cooks, executioners.

This court was organized like the Eastern courts. Its arrangement promoted conflicts between the intimates and officials in a struggle for influence and authority.

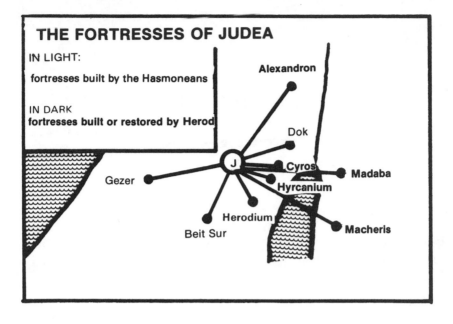

THE FORTRESSES OF JUDEA

IN LIGHT:

fortresses built by the Hasmoneans

IN DARK
fortresses built or restored by Herod

Alexandron

Dok

Gezer

J

Cyros

Madaba

Hyrcanium

Herodium

Beit Sur

Macheris

Chapter 8

Herod's Sons

The story of Herod and his sons is complex. Herod's power had made Rome uneasy, and so, in agreement with the emperor, the old king divided his kingdom into three parts for his sons, Archelaus, Antipas and Philip. Rome accepted this but refused to allow them to use the title of king and placed the three under the supervision of the governor of Syria.

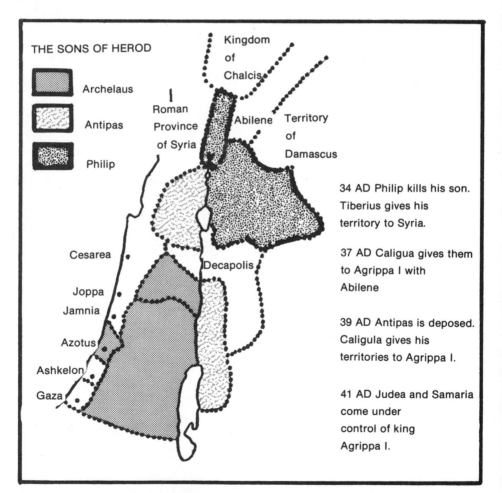

THE SONS OF HEROD

- Archelaus
- Antipas
- Philip

Kingdom of Chalcis

Roman Province of Syria

Abilene Territory of Damascus

Cesarea

Joppa

Jamnia

Azotus

Ashkelon

Gaza

Decapolis

34 AD Philip kills his son. Tiberius gives his territory to Syria.

37 AD Caligua gives them to Agrippa I with Abilene

39 AD Antipas is deposed. Caligula gives his territories to Agrippa I.

41 AD Judea and Samaria come under control of king Agrippa I.

Archelaus received Judea, Samaria, Idumea and, on the coast, Joppa, Caesarea, Jamnia and Azoth. He began by putting down a rebellion in Jerusalem and eliminating pretenders to the throne. He went to Rome to obtain the title of king. Jews and Samaritans made complaints about him.

Archelaus was deposed and exiled to the current town of Vienne, near Lyon, France, where he died in 18 A.D. His territory was administered by a Roman procurator, Agrippa I.

Antipas received Galilee and Perea. He undertook a great deal of construction in his lands and built Tiberias in Galilee.

He wanted to marry his niece, the former wife of Philip (cf. Mt. 14:4). His wife pushed him to become king.

He reassumed the name of Herod Antipas in 6 A.D., and was a contemporary of Christ. In 39 A.D. Caligula deposed him and exiled him to what is now St. Bertrand de Comminge in the Pyrenees.

He was replaced by Agrippa I, brother of Herodias, and grandson of Herod the Great.

Philip received the northern part of the country: Golan, Auranitis, Batanea, Iturea, Trachonitis. He built Caesarea Philippi (Mt. 15) and had a peaceful reign.

He married Salome, the daughter of Herodias. In 34 A.D. he died without a child and Tiberias reattached his territory to the province of Syria.

In 37 A.D. Caligula gave these territories to Agrippa I, with the Abilene.

Agrippa I had lived in Rome. He was a friend of Caligula and of Claudius, whom he helped become emperor. The latter named him king and gave him, in 41, all the territories which had been administered by Herod the Great. Agrippa dealt peacefully with the Pharisees, killing James (Acts 12:2) in Jerusalem. He was not careless about Jewish customs, did much building and sought peace. Outside Palestine he was very active and disregarded Jewish customs. He wanted to rebuild the ramparts of Jerusalem but Claudius stopped him. He died in 44 at Caesarea (Acts 12:20–23).

By 44, Palestine was thus a single Roman province.

Agrippa II, 50–108, the son of Agrippa I, was loyal to Rome. Claudius gave him the territories of Philip (in 53) and Nero, and part of those of Herod Antipas (Acts 25–26). He finished the temple; eighteen thousand workers were thereupon unemployed. He put them to work paving the streets.

The Herodians

This group was opposed to Jesus (Mk. 3:16; 12:3; Mt. 22:16). It is not really known exactly whom they represented. Possibly:

1. Jews who were partisans of Herod the Great and very active in the beginning of his reign, opposed to the Zealots.

2. Or the group who admired Herod the Great almost to the point of considering him the Messiah—possibly less strict Essenes who had made accommodations to Herod's policy.

3. Or partisans and agents of Herod Antipas.

4. Or more probably the group of Sadducees who were partisans of Herod and had remained loyal to his family, Herod having been able to hold them.

Chapter 9

Levites

The name of this tribe comes from Levi, the patriarch and one of the twelve sons of Jacob. Originally the twelve tribes of Israel were completely independent, but when they united to form a people, about 1100 B.C., each tribe showed its connection with the others by tracing its origin back to one of the twelve brothers who had been sons of a single father.

When the land was distributed in Palestine, the tribe of Levi received none of its own; instead, for its living, it received the tithes of each tribe's territories, the Lord being considered as its inheritance.

1. Origins of the Levites

The history is not entirely clear.

We know that Palestine had several places of worship. All of these honored the one God, EL, under different titles or designations.

Sites of the sanctuaries	Patriarch associated	Title under which God (EL) was honored	Reference
Penuel (east of Jerusalem)	Jacob	God appears; he sees	Gen. 12:8
then Bethel	Jacob	House (ladder, tower) of EL, the Omnipotent of Jacob. (Gen. 48:24)	
Shechem	Israel	EL of the Covenant (El-Berit) Rock, Shepherd of Israel (Gen. 49:24)	Gen. 12:6
Shiloh	Judges Joshua	"Watered place"; God of the ark Egyptian influences (?)	Jgs. 21:19–24
Beersheba	Isaac	El-Olam, the Eternal God Parent (Gen. 31–42)	Gen. 26:23
Mambre Hebron	Abraham	El-Shaddar, God of the mountain	Gen. 18:1
Jerusalem	Melchisedech	El-Eluon, the Most High	Gen. 14:19
Wells of El-King	Ishmael	God sees (Lahai sees)	Gen. 16:14

There were other temples at Dan, Arad, etc.

When the kings, particularly after Solomon, unified all these places of worship into a single central one, the sanctuary at Jerusalem, the question remained: What was to be done with the clergy from the high places? Gradually they were attached to the temple at Jerusalem as assistants to the priests. They did not take part in the sacrificial worship and even incurred the death penalty if they approached the altar or entered the court reserved for the priests. The priests were descendants of Aaron and of the high priest of the family of Zadok, Solomon's priest.

Other groups sometimes ended up as Levites: for example, descendants of slaves, even foreigners, were given to the temple and to the clergy; these were called "the given."

2. Functions

Levites were occupied with temple services, and two particular types of work were assigned to them:

a. Singing and music

One group accompanied the daily morning and evening ceremonies. They stood in the temple, between the court of the Israelites and the court of the priests.

b. Servants of the temple (somewhat like sacristans)

They helped the priests put on and take off their vestments, and cleaned the temple, except the two places forbidden to them, the sanctuary and the court of the priests. They were the temple police; they guarded the gates and kept watch day and night. (Only priests guarded the sanctuary.) These temple-servants were the police who arrested Jesus (Mk. 14:18; Jn. 7:32, 45–46).

A Levite chief inspected the night guard and was perhaps the head gatekeeper. These police had no official uniforms; they numbered about 9,600.

3. Organization

A chief Levite lived in Jerusalem and was fairly rich. Like the priests, the Levites were divided into twenty-four sections per week, each with a section head. There were four permanent positions in the temple for each series of duties.

Re the integration of former priests:
"And every one who is left in your house shall come to implore him for a piece of silver or a loaf of bread, and shall say, 'Put me, I pray you, in one of the priest's places, that I may eat a morsel of bread.' "
1 Sam. 2:36; cf. 2 Kgs. 23:9

a. **Singers and musicians:**
   Two chief supervisors
   Two heads of music
   Two heads of choir
b. **Servants of the temple:**
   Two chief supervisors
   One head gateman
   One head guard

One was born a Levite; it was an hereditary right, especially guarded by singers and musicians. A young man of a Levite family was examined in the hall of the Sanhedrin when he was thirty years old: he could have no physical defect, his genealogy was studied, and he had to marry within his own rank. Then he was accepted as a Levite.

In fact, the Levites formed a layer of the population which was very poor, especially in the country. Many were unable to live on tithes and had to work, often as scribes. Very many lived in intolerable conditions and were deeply resentful of the priests, who were generally better provided for. They constituted a group that was easily aroused for anything which, it seemed, would help them out of their misery.

Cult Places

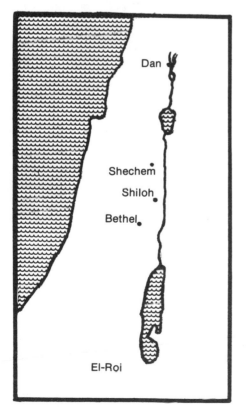

Chapter 10

Manuscripts and Writing

The Bible is today the most widely sold book in the world. From 1954 to 1964, more than nineteen hundred translations of the Bible were made. The Bible now exists in almost all written languages, and the translations are constantly being improved. In 1964, for example, the Bible was translated two hundred and twenty-eight times in thirty-three countries, and in 1972, it was translated one hundred and nine times (compared to sixty-two translations of Marx in the same year). These figures include translations of the New Testament only.

1. *History of the Texts*

The New Testament is a collection of Christian writings in which the Church recognizes and strengthens its faith. Over several centuries, when it had meditated on them, the Church chose and retained the present texts. After the persecutions had ended, the Christian communities exchanged lists of the texts they had retained. The official list of books is commonly called the canon.

When a copy of the New Testament is bought in a bookstore, it will include:

Four Gospels and the Acts of the Apostles;

Thirteen Epistles of St. Paul and eight other Epistles;

The Book of Revelation.

This is a total of twenty-seven books.

All English versions of the New Testament are translations. Where do they come from? They come from the *Greek text* which was established in the sixteenth century (with editions by Erasmus in 1516 and Robert Estienne in 1546) and widely distributed thanks to the printing press. The text comes from the best Greek manuscripts preserved in libraries, which were recovered and compiled during the Renaissance.

Before the printing press, there were:

1. Parchments. The word itself comes from the Turkish city of Pergamum. A parchment is the skin of a sheep, goat or calf, carefully cleaned, tanned and treated with chalk. Parchments are kept either in rolls or in volumes, in which the sheets of skin are sewn together like a book.

From the fourth to the ninth century, parchments were written in majuscule or large letters; they are called "uncials," a word which means "big as a thumb." There are one hundred and fifty-seven large uncial parchments.

There are also hundreds of parchments in existence written in miniscule letters—hence their name "miniscules." They date from the ninth century to the Renaissance.

2. Papyri. Papyrus manuscripts, made from a reed which grew in marshes, are difficult to preserve. The material cannot take dryness which makes it crumble, or humidity which makes it decay. We have thirty-five important papyri and a great number of fragments. The oldest is a short passage from Chapter 18 of St. John, 2.3 by 3.6 inches in size, dating from about 130 A.D. It was copied forty years after the composition of the Gospel by St. John in Asia Minor.

One of the reasons that there are so few manuscripts is that in 303 the Emperor Diocletian (284–305) ordered the destruction of churches and the burning of Christian books. Nevertheless we have manuscripts of passages of the New Testament dating from the third and fourth centuries in all the languages of the Roman Empire.

2. *Status of the Manuscripts*

There are one hundred and ninety-two extant manuscripts of the New Testament. By comparison there are extant:

    1 Tacitus—Latin—55–120 A.D.

    50 Aeschylus—Greek—525–426 B.C.

    100 Cicero—Latin—106–43 B.C.

    100 Sophocles—Greek—496–406 B.C.

The first complete extant manuscript dates from one century after the composition of the last Gospel (about 90 A.D.). For other ancient writ-

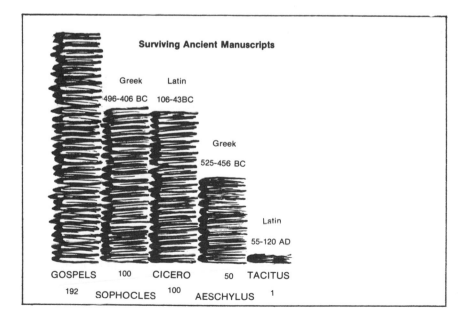

Surviving Ancient Manuscripts

Greek   Latin

496-406 BC   106-43BC

Greek

525-456 BC

Latin

55-120 AD

GOSPELS   100   CICERO   50   TACITUS

192   SOPHOCLES   100   AESCHYLUS   1

ings the time span between the writer's life and the first extant manuscript is as follows:

4 centuries for Vergil—Latin—70–19 B.C.

12 centuries for Demosthenes—Greek—384–322 B.C.

16 centuries for Euripides—Greek—480–406 B.C.

3. *Use of the Manuscripts*

There is no original text in existence—and how would we know if it were the original? There are only copies.

The manuscripts are classified by families, having each been copied by a single group. Among the texts, there are innumerable differences, which are called *variants*. For the Greek text of the New Testament there are as many as 250,000 variants (more than all the words) which run from a change of a letter to an occasional omission of a paragraph (e.g., Mk. 16:9–20). Nineteen variants are considered important but only one is doctrinal in content (Lk. 22:19b–20a). These big variants are indicated in the notes of editions. Specialists compare these variants, explain the differences and choose the best attested solution, that is, the most frequent or most certain. The most difficult variant is often the truest: a copyist may have simplified what he did not understand.

1. Papyrus grew in marshes, having stalks seven to ten feet in length. It was used to make rope, sandals, and boats. From the time of the last Egyptian dynasty (3100–2890 B.C.) it was apparently used for making paper.

2. The outer rind was removed and the pith cut into fine strips.

3. Two layers of these were placed crosswise on a flat stone and covered with a protective cloth.

4. They were then beaten with a hammer for about an hour and a half to make the two layers stick together.

5. The dried sheet was polished with a rounded stone. The edges were cut; the papyrus sheet was ready.

Chapter 11

Marriage

A village usually contained members of a single clan. As administrators of the village community, the elders constituted the group's memory, registering sales, births, and marriages in their heads. People generally married within the clan.

The family was part of the clan. It contained the grandparents, parents, brothers, sisters and cousins. (There was no word to designate cousin.) The family was considered the fraternal house (Mk. 6:3–4).

People usually married very early. A girl could be given in marriage at the age of twelve and a half. The parents of the two young people arranged the marriage, in order to protect the property of the family, that is, the clan.

Because the girl who was marrying had done work in her family's house, the family of the future husband compensated for her departure by paying money or rendering services. This payment was called the *mohar*; and it became the woman's property if her husband died or if she was repudiated. The two fathers arranged this contract. In addition, the fiancé offered the woman a dowry.

Betrothal

If the couple was too young or if there was another reason for delaying the wedding, there would be a betrothal. A betrothal lasted for one year, but it was a very serious undertaking. The fiancé promised to provide the woman's food, lodging and clothing. If the man died, his betrothed was considered a widow.

The Wedding

A wedding was a great family festivity, offered to the whole family, the village, guests and passers-by. Banquets, songs, and dances followed one after another continuously for a whole week. There was no civil or religious ceremony outside the house, but at the annual pilgrimage to the temple the young couple offered a sacrifice and received a blessing.

The spectacle began on the wedding morning. The bride wore a long veil covering her hair and dress, and her friends fastened a cincture around her gown. At night, the groom would lift off the veil and unfasten the cincture.

The procession moved from the groom's house, preceded by musicians; to the rhythm of tambourines and the clapping of hands, the men danced as they advanced. They sang the praises of the clan, of the families, and of the groom. First came the father, followed by the father-in-law, the village elders, and finally the groom, surrounded by friends of his own age. It sometimes happened that the groom was delayed if the final discussions about the contract had not been completed—and it was a point of honor to drag them out.

Before leaving her house, the bride had to lament, to show that she was being torn from her home. All the women wept and wailed. The maid of honor repaired the bride's appearance and she finally left the house, accompanied by her unmarried friends.

When the women had joined the men's procession, all turned toward the home of the groom's father. The dancing and music resumed, accompanied by the joyful shouts of the women, with their hands lightly beating their lips. The singers improvised couplets praising the betrothed and their families.

When the wedding party reached the house of the groom's father, he blessed the bride. Then the two young people exchanged their vows. After a cup of wine was blessed and they thanked God (see prayer below), the young husband, and then the wife, drank from the cup and threw it down.

The festivities continued, with more singing and dancing. The bride stayed with her companions in a separate room where she received

---

Prayer at the marriage ceremony
Blessed be the Lord our God, king of the universe,
who created the fruit of the vine!
Blessed be the Lord our God, king of the universe,
who created man!
Blessed be the Lord our God, king of the universe,
who created man in his image!
who willed to give him one like himself and a mode of life,
who made for man a house for all time—a woman!
Blessed be the Lord our God, king of the universe,
who gladdens the newly married!
Blessed be the Lord our God, king of the universe,
who created joy and happiness,
the new husband and the bride,
love, fraternity, feasts,
happiness, peace and society!
May the Lord our God make resound
in all the cities of Judea,
in the squares of Jerusalem,
the cries of the new groom and his bride,
the music of the wedding dinner
and the sound of the young people's instruments!
Blessed be the Lord who gives happiness
to the new husband and to the bride
and will make them prosper!
Celebrate the Lord for he is good
and eternal is his love.
May joy increase!
May plaints and sighs be banished!

guests. Outside, the groom paid honor to each guest, and he remained with them until very late before going to his bride. When he came, her companions withdrew and extinguished their lamps. It was absolutely required that the wife be a virgin.

Polygamy

Polygamy was authorized by the law but existed only in several cases: among the affluent who could pay several dowries, or, on the contrary, among the poor who could not pay a dowry. It existed in about ten percent of the families, but was forbidden at Qumran.

Polygamy was based on the false idea that there are more women than men and that women must be looked after. (Actually, about 104 girls are born to 100 boys, and the number levels out around the age of twenty.) Two conditions are necessary for polygamy: 1. men must marry late; 2. female celibacy must be unacceptable. Nonetheless, polygamy was dying out in Palestine in the first century.

The Jewish Woman

Women were considered inferior to men, generally did not take part in public life (though one was a queen), and were not called as witnesses in court. In the temple, they stayed in the women's court, which was the most remote, and in the synagogue, they sat with the children and slaves. They could not read there or offer a prayer, but the situation was more liberal among Jews living abroad. Less study of the law was required of women than of men.

Women ceased to be considered children at twelve and could marry at twelve and a half. These six months of adolescence were reserved for the father's right to hire out a daughter as a servant or to sell her as a slave for seven years. Most women were married between twelve and fourteen. The husband could repudiate a wife, but the reverse was impossible. (Mark 10:12 was written for Romans, in whose case wives could obtain a divorce.) If a woman was repudiated, her dowry was returned to her. Divorces could be obtained for serious causes (though adultery was punishable by death) or simply because she no longer gave pleasure (Mt. 19:3).

Bearing many children, the Jewish woman aged rapidly, and the house and work in the fields were her lot. A sterile woman was despised. When the Jewish woman went out, she covered her head—no one spoke to her or could stare at her (Mt. 5: 28; Jn. 4:27)—but at home she was often in command.

Jesus acted much more freely than the law and included women friends among his disciples (Lk. 8:1–2).

To marry a stranger is to drink from a jug;
To marry a girl from one's clan is to drink from a spring.

Hebrew proverb

Chapter 12

The Messiah

The word "messiah" comes from a Hebrew word which means "unction" or anointing with oil. This word was translated into Greek by *christ*, a word with the same root as chrism: oil and perfume for anointing. In the Bible, kings and high priests were anointed and sometimes both altars and prophets were also.

This anointing was meant to show that the vivifying power of God had taken possession of the person so marked to the very depths of his being.

1. Origin

The idea of a messiah was very widely diffused. It is found in a great many religions, and even in modern times in numerous social groups. This idea is linked to:

a. an awareness, felt by the group, of a lack of something they seriously need;

b. the hope and expectation of a providential man who will draw them from this situation;

c. the survival and expansion of this group from within which the messiah will arise;

d. the judgment of enemies and their present or future destruction.

The idea of the messiah is based on a binary logic: good/evil, present/future, enemy/friend, etc. When intervening in a catastrophic situation, the messiah, who is the envoy of a god, hero, political genius, etc., brings an exceptional force to bear which turns the situation around; he is thus considered a sacred person.

Its results are likewise doubled:

a. Messianic thought activates and mobilizes hope, keeps it going and prevents complete demoralization.

b. However, it is quite ready to accept, in an emotional unreflective way, the first person who arouses it. Salvation does not come from the group but from outside, through a man with extraordinary endowments. The whole problem is to know whether a group thus mobilized will find itself robbed of victory.

In fact, its logic is not twofold but threefold:

a. A situation of oppression

b. leads to intervention by a superior man,

c. resulting in a situation of abundance.

2. Process

The following sequence flows immediately from the above: the messiah is characterized by the situation from which he must draw the oppressed group. The group's need dictates its hope and the figure of the messiah. Therefore, the messiah will bring to the future the good which was missing in the past. His role is that of preserver, but in reverse: what was lacking is now present. Even though this process involves a revolution, it creates nothing: the order of distribution of goods is changed but the logic remains the same. In this light, reread the Magnificat (Lk. 1:47–55).

We can find several types of messiah in the Bible:

FELT NEED	Liberated being	To have a big country	To have a holy priest	To have a national prophet
Past model	Moses in the exodus	David's kingdom	The assassinated high priest Onias (2 Macc. 4:30)	Elias (cf. Deut. 18:15)
Model hoped for	A political liberator	A son of David	A just priest and head of the people (Qumran)	A prophet proclaiming the Messiah
Revelations of a messiah	Many (cf. Acts 5:36–37)	For some it was Herod (in time)	Community at Qumran prepares to receive him	Said of Jesus (Jn. 9:17)

3. What the Bible Adds

The Bible modifies this process in two ways:

a. It proclaims one "like a son of man" (Dn. 7:13–14). This being, hidden in God and held in reserve, will bring the presence of God. The commentaries on this text at the time of Christ compared this son of man to the true Adam, but this teaching was reserved to the scribes. Later, it was picked up by Paul.

b. It speaks of a "suffering servant" (Is. 53); like Jeremiah, salvation comes from another line: a just man through love delivers himself for others and bears the weight of misery. He breaks the logic of oppressed/oppressor by the introduction of the logic of love.

4. Jesus Christ

He was given the various titles of the messiah in turn, especially that of "Son of God," which was the royal title meaning "protected by God." He refused to be seen as a type of the messiah (Mk. 8:29–30) and he only accepted it during his passion when he gave himself up (Mk. 14:61–62). Jesus preferred the title "Son of Man" which refers directly to the presence of God in his people. He particularly liked the idea of the suffering servant, one chosen by God to give up his life (Mt. 13:17; Mk. 10:45; Jn. 10:18). In relation to the conditions and concepts of his time, Jesus was indeed a messiah but in another way. He followed another logic. He was messiah, but in the Father's way. That is how he opened the way to his recognition as truly the Son of God (Mk. 15:19).

Chapter 13

Palestine

The name of the country comes from the Philistines, who, however, occupied only a small portion of it. The Philistines came from the north by sea, pushed out by migrations from eastern Europe. (See the chapter on Canaan.)

Blocked by Egypt, they established themselves on the coast in the twelfth century B.C. and tried to move into the interior of the country. Because they were enemies of the Israelite tribes, they often supported the Syrian powers, and the tribes solidified against them.

1. Appearance of the Country

Palestine is a trapezoid, bounded on the east by the Jordan, on the west by the Mediterranean Sea, on the north by the spur of Mount Hermon (9380 ft.) and on the south by the Negeb desert (a coastal band twenty-five miles wide in the south and three miles wide in the north). There are three successive regions formed by mountainous plateaus separated by plains.

To the east, because of a very deep fault, the Jordan valley prolongs the gorge which begins at the African Great Lakes and extends along the

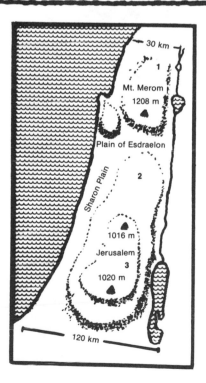

1. Upper and Lower Galilee
2. Plateau of Samaria
3. Plateau of Judea

course of the Nile to the Gulf of Aqaba. The elevation falls 3,300 feet in fifteen miles on an east-west axis.

Palestine is a small country, somewhat less than fifteen thousand square miles. Distances within it are very short: for example, from Jerusalem to Nazareth is eighty-seven miles; from Jerusalem to Beersheba, fifty miles. But the mountains hinder travel.

2. *Climate*

Palestine has a Mediterranean climate, warmer in the east, more arid in the south. There is a great difference in temperature between day and night, as much as seventy to seventy-five degrees between noon and midnight. There are essentially two seasons, summer and winter. Spring and autumn are very short. It snows in winter.

The wind blows from the east and is very cold in winter, and from the desert comes a dry, warm wind (the Khamsin). Rain falls in October and March. Otherwise, except for occasional torrential showers, dryness is always a problem. Streams (wadi) are almost always dry in the summer. The Jordan, by exception, is always high at harvest time because of the snows melting on Lebanon.

At the time of Christ, the mountains were covered with forests and between the mountains and the coastal plain lay a moor.

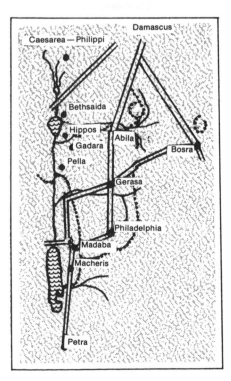

3. Population

Palestine alone had about 500,000 inhabitants in Christ's time. Adding the Decapolis, Idumea and the non-Jewish population, the figure was almost a million. Jerusalem itself had 20,000 to 25,000 inhabitants, with another 5,000 scattered in the nearby villages. By comparison, Antioch in Syria had 500,000 inhabitants and Alexandria in Egypt had 600,000.

The language was no longer Hebrew, which was used only in the temple liturgy. From the time of the Babylonian exile, it had been Aramaic, the language of the nomads to the east. One form of Aramaic is still spoken in a few Syrian villages. The southern part of the country spoke Arabic, and Greek was commonly used in the cities along the Sea of Galilee (cf. Jn. 12:20–21; Philip, for example, was a Greek name). Greek was the language of merchants and of educated people.

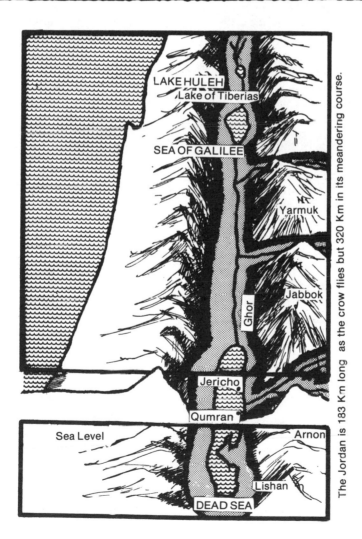

LAKE HULEH
Lake of Tiberias
SEA OF GALILEE
Yarmuk
Jabbok
Ghor
Jericho
Qumran
Sea Level
Arnon
Lishan
DEAD SEA

The Jordan is 183 Km long as the crow flies but 320 Km in its meandering course.

4. Regions (from south to north)

a. Idumea

This is the Greco-Roman name of the small kingdom called "Edom" in Aramaic. This kingdom had possessed the whole Negeb in the sixth century. The territory was conquered in 126 B.C. by the high priest John Hyrcanus, and the Romans allowed him regional autonomy. In principle, the people were attached to Judaism, but they maintained their distinctive characteristics. This was Herod the Great's country. Sheep were raised there.

b. The Free Cities

A certain number of ports or cities along coastal routes were successively autonomous, subject to Herod the Great, or attached directly to the legate of Syria—for example, Gaza and Ascalon.

c. Judea, Samaria, Perea

After Herod's time the name Judea designated the district of Jerusalem and the coastal plain to the north of the Roman capital of Caesarea. On a drier plateau to the south was Samaria, whose capital was Sebaste-Samaria, a richer and more verdant region. Perea was acquired by the high priests in the first century before Christ. Its capitals were Amathonte and Betharampha, which were also called Livias in honor of the Empress Livia-Julia.

d. Galilee

The name comes from the district of "Galil." Upper Galilee has an average altitude of two thousand feet. The highest point was Mount Merom (2025 ft.). The district was inhabited by a single type of people, basically Jewish but mixed with peoples from the north. It was divided into large villages. The soil was chalky with impenetrable brush, but it provided supplementary farming for shepherds.

Lower Galilee, with an average altitude of eight hundred and twenty-five feet, was highly cultivated, and was a passageway for travel.

As for the Sea of Galilee its shores were heavily populated, with many Greeks. The region was settled by people who had been displaced in the first century before Christ. The sea was thirteen miles long by seven and a half miles wide, with an average depth of 165 to 235 feet, reaching 825 feet in its center. Rich in fish, the water was slightly salty. The water could rise thirty-five feet with rains and swells. It was called "Kinnereth" (the zither). Strong winds blew down from the mountains.

The Jordan

The name means "descender." It falls from an altitude of 665 feet above sea level to 1,400 feet below, at the Dead Sea. This torrent has its source in three rivers which meet in the marshes of Lake Huleh to form a single watercourse with an average flow of 3,600 cubic feet per second. Within ten miles it reaches the Sea of Galilee, having fallen 945 feet over that length, from 225 feet above sea level to 705 below. It is never navigable. The valley ranges in width from 1¼ or 2 miles to 12½ miles at Jericho. This bushy valley is called the "Ghor."

Lake Huleh was a marshy country.
The mountain people spilled over onto the plain.

e. Decapolis.

These were groups of free cities united among themselves, varying in number but usually about ten. Later they were attached to the legate of Syria. They were predominantly Greek; only Hippos was largely Jewish.

f. Trachonitis and the northern regions

This region of volcanic rock, southwest of Damascus, was infested by brigands—a land of pasturage and grain crops.

5. *The Diaspora*

The word comes from Greek and means "dispersion." It designated the Jewish people living outside Palestine, numbering more than six million.

a. Origin

In every period of their history Jews went abroad to trade or were taken off as prisoners. The various military expeditions of the Pharaohs and of Syrian and Mesopotamian princes made it possible for Jews to settle abroad. With the conquest of Samaria in 721 B.C. and then of Jerusalem (596–587), thousands of Jews were deported to Babylon. A number remained in Mesopotamia even after the Edict of Cyrus in 538. Centers developed under the Persian and Greek empires; while they all remained authentically Jewish, the language varied. In Egypt and Syria, Greek was spoken; in Italy, Latin was the language, while Aramaic was kept in Mesopotamia and Iran.

b. Organization

While Roman families began to have fewer children, the Jews continued to value larger families. To be considered a Jew, a man had to be the son of a Jewish mother, to be circumcised and to be brought up according to the law.

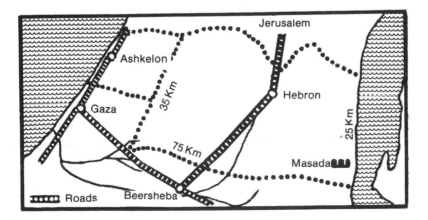

51

Jewish settlers were sometimes farmers, sometimes soldiers, (there was a Jewish garrison, for example, at Elephantine in Egypt). Most often they lived in cities, where they gathered into a single quarter. They were often organized. In Alexandria, the Jewish community had a "senate," a sort of free municipality, with its president, secretary and council of elders, and Emperor Augustus approved this organization. Ordinarily, Jewish laws were recognized by the states; and the Jewish population, as resident foreigners (metis then had no perjorative connation), was protected and kept its internal autonomy as regards worship, language and law. The sabbath was respected; it was even a reason for not being enrolled in the army in the Middle East. Jews could acquire the title of Roman citizens (Acts 22:25–29).

They continued to be responsible to the high priest in Jerusalem and displayed great solidarity. They had synagogues with a president of the synagogue and a council of elders, and sometimes a priest and a lector-translator of Scripture. They paid a tax of a half-shekel yearly. Silver was taken to the temple at Jerusalem by a messenger protected by law. At Alexandria, the Bible was translated into Greek (285–246 B.C.). Religious parties had their ramifications in the diaspora. Jews living abroad had their synagogue in Jerusalem (Acts 6:9).

c. Reactions

Antisemitism existed. Circumcision, the refusal to eat certain foods, and keeping the sabbath became matters of derision. Many writers made

---

The Dead Sea
50 by 10 miles, to the north of the Lisan peninsula. Average depth 135 ft.; in the south, 35 ft. Water very salty, sulphurous. Much asphalt. No life. 1,300 ft. below level of the Mediterranean.

Air Karim is not mentioned in the New Testament
Bethania on the Jordan (where John baptized) cannot be located with certainty.
Dalmanutha (Mk. 8:10) is unknown.
Emmaus: two places can claim to be the site of Lk. 24.
Gerasenes (Lk. 8:26): if this is not Ferasa, no one knows where it is.
Gomorrah and Sodom: probable sites; the cities have disappeared.
Magadan (Mt. 15:39) is unknown.
Salim, where John baptized, is unknown.

fun of the Jews, and they were charged with atheism because they would not sacrifice to idols.

Riots sometimes broke out in the big cities—for example, in Alexandria in 58 A.D.—with many deaths. Also the Palestinian revolt in 66 A.D. provoked the massacre of Jews in Antioch and Caesarea.

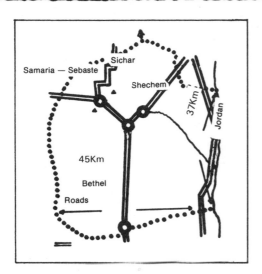

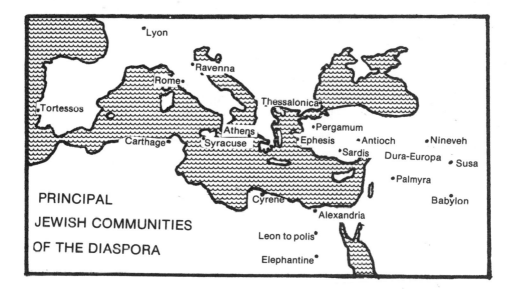

PRINCIPAL

JEWISH COMMUNITIES

OF THE DIASPORA

Major New Testament city names

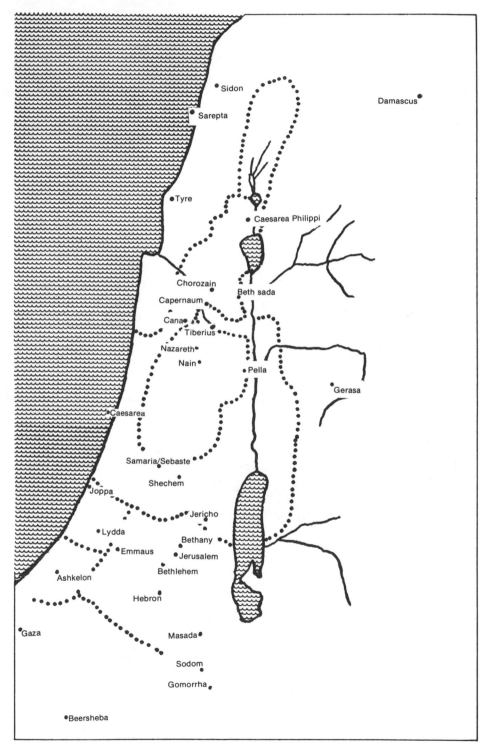

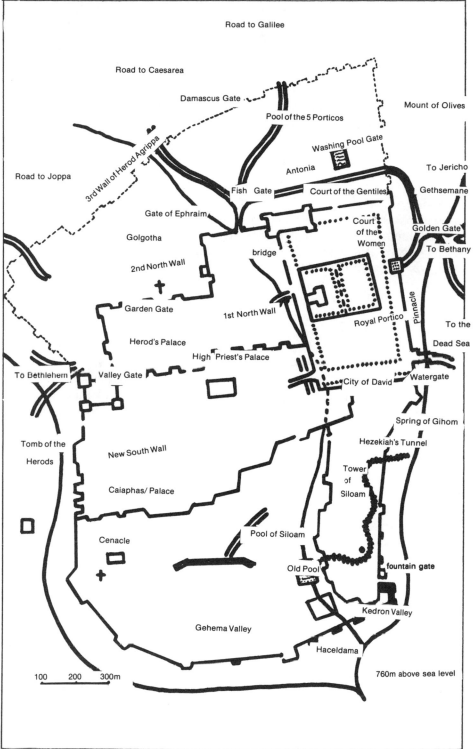

Road to Galilee

Road to Caesarea

Damascus Gate

Pool of the 5 Porticos

Mount of Olives

Washing Pool Gate

Antonia

To Jericho

Road to Joppa

3rd Wall of Herod Agrippa

Fish Gate

Court of the Gentiles

Gethsemane

Gate of Ephraim

Court of the Women

Golden Gate

Golgotha

bridge

To Bethany

2nd North Wall

Garden Gate

1st North Wall

Royal Portico

To the

Dead Sea

Herod's Palace

Pinnacle

High Priest's Palace

To Bethlehem

Valley Gate

City of David

Watergate

Spring of Gihom

Tomb of the
Herods

New South Wall

Hezekiah's Tunnel

Tower
of
Siloam

Caiaphas/ Palace

Cenacle

Pool of Siloam

Old Pool

fountain gate

Kedron Valley

Gehema Valley

Haceldama

100   200   300m

760m above sea level

55

Chapter 14

The Pharisees

The Gospel often speaks of the Pharisees, but what does the word mean? The word seems to come from the verb "parasch," to separate, to make a separate group. It designated both a *political party* and a *religious tendency*.

1. *History*

After the death of Alexander the Great in 323 B.C. his empire was divided among his generals. One of them established a kingdom in Syria with Antioch as its capital—present-day Ankara in Turkey. Antiochus Epiphanus, a descendant, wanted to impose on the Jews laws inspired by Greece. It was then that devout people, who were committed to the Jewish law, joined a revolt led by Mattathias Maccabeus and his partisans.

The Jewish revolt was successful, and these devout people regrouped in religious and political centers with the scribes, who were laymen, in associations intended to insure respect for the law and cult. Their very great influence around 135–115 B.C. reinforced the cohesiveness of their groups. Their political influence declined after 63 B.C. with the Roman occupation, but, as members of the Sanhedrin, they maintained a real influence on the courts and in religion. Herod the Great took them into account and avoided direct confrontations with them, even more so because their ideology reached into the domestic side of the court and the royal harem. Nevertheless, he required two oaths of fidelity from them: to himself and to Augustus. When they refused—and a first-century Jewish historian estimated that more than six thousand did refuse—Herod killed many of them. Their political role passed into the hands of the Sadducees until the revolt in 66–70 A.D. After the seizure of Jerusalem by Titus in 70 A.D. and the burning of the temple, the Pharisees be-

Origin of the Pharisees
"Then there were united with them a company of Hasideans, mighty warriors of Israel, everyone who offered himself willingly to the law" (I Macc. 2:42).

came the champions of a national renaissance. Since the Gospels were written after 70, there was a tendency to confuse the Pharisees and the scribes: these two groups were distinct, though some scribes were Pharisees.

2. Social Position

To become a Pharisee it was sufficient, after a probationary period of between a month and a year, to promise to keep the rules of the association regarding ritual purity, fasting, tithing and other religious practices (cf. Lk. 18:11–12).

They recruited members from all layers of society. Tradesmen, artisans, priests, scribes—all were part of the group. The temple priests were closely linked to the movement because they wished to impose on all Jews their own rules of ritual purity. Often these were ordinary people, virtuous, irreproachable, poor, and disinterested. They were concerned with liberating the people and helping the poor, but they used their charitable actions visibly as a means of propaganda (Mt. 6:2).

Their ideal of purity led them to condemn the conservative nobility who followed Herod, the Sadducees who accepted the illegitimate high priest, and common people, "the people of the land," whose fidelity to the law and payment of tithes they doubted.

The Pharisees enjoyed great favor and were influential in the synagogues. Paul was a Pharisee (Acts 24:4; Phil. 3:5).

3. Doctrine

Banded in associations with different leanings, the Pharisees gathered in small groups, usually for a common meal on Friday. Their leaders were often the more educated scribes. The ideal was to make Israel a holy people "like the priests" (Ex. 19:6), aloof from sinners (Lev. 11:45). Their rigorous prescriptions (Mk. 7:3–4) led them to avoid all contact with sinners and with those whose conduct might lead to less strict obedience to the law. Jesus shocked them by rejecting these barriers (Mk. 2:15–17).

The Pharisees' style of life is neither easy nor delightful, but simple. They hold strongly to what they believe they should embrace. They so greatly honor old men that they will not even contradict them. They attribute everything which happens to fate, without, however, taking away man's power to consent thereto, so that, while everything happens by the will of God, it still depends on our will whether we act in a virtuous or evil way. They believe that souls are immortal, that they are judged in another world and rewarded or punished according to what they have been in this one, virtuous or evil, and that the latter remain eternally in that life as prisoners and the former return to this one. Through this belief they have acquired such authority among the people that they follow their advice in everything regarding the worship of God and the solemn prayers which are made to him. Also entire cities give witness to their virtue, their way of life and their discourse.

Flavius Josephus, Jewish Antiquities, 18, 2.

In addition to the written law, to which the Sadducees adhered strictly, the Pharisees accepted the oral tradition, even when it was extreme (Mt. 15:1–20). But their acceptance of the oral tradition still allowed them to make adaptations, to work around it. They professed the equality and freedom of all men and believed in the immortality of the soul and the resurrection (Acts 23:6–10). Disillusioned by Herod's family, they pinned their messianic hope on the observance of the law: fidelity would hasten the coming of the Messiah. Pride was their stumbling block, the pride of considering themselves just. The best of them recognized this. They distinguished seven kinds of Pharisees and tried themselves to be "the Pharisees of love" whose model was Abraham. For them it was not enough to wear a tiny leather box on the forehead containing a verse of the law (phylactery) or a verse fastened to the left sleeve (near the heart) with a leather strap: they realized that God wants the worship of the heart.

Jesus was very close to this last group. He was condemned in the name of the divine authority which he exercised. The Pharisees, however, were not present in the accounts of the passion; this sort of trial was the domain of the priests and the Sadducees.

The seven kinds of Pharisees:
1. *The self-interested.*
2. *The one who gives himself airs.*
3. *The "hit on the head" who walks with downcast eyes so as not to see a woman and bumps into the wall.*
4. *The "pile driver" who walks bent over in outward piety, as if he were always driving down a heavy stake.*
5. *The one who runs to his duty.*
6. *The one who performs a good deed every day.*
7. *The one who acts out of respect and love for God.*

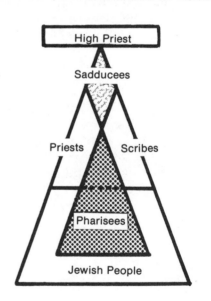

Chapter 15

Political Situation

It is difficult to explain the political situation in present-day categories. Several principles of classification are possible, according to different criteria.

A. **Religious classification**

 1. High Priests
 2. Priests
 3. Levites
 4. Good Israelites (pure by birth
    and observant of the law)
 5. "Stained" Israelites
 6. Proselytes
 7. Slaves
 8. Samaritans

However, the economic situation of the lower ranking priests and the Levites and the place of the scribes is not shown in this chart.

B. **Classification with respect to tradition**
   Separation was made through the acceptance of the idea of development.

 1. *Temper:*   very conservative
    Members: high priests
                Sadducees
                elders
                Zealots

 2. *Temper:*   conservative
    Members: priests
                scribes of Sadduceean view

 3. *Temper:*   opportunist
    Members: Herodians
                some scribes

 4. *Temper:*   open, accepting oral tradition
    Members: priests
                scribes
                Pharisees

 5. *Temper:*   very open
    Members: a few scribes

C. Classification according to the Romans
1. Collaborators
   Herodians
   Sanhedrin circles (compromise required)
   Publicans (through their work)
2. Hostile
   Pharisees and most of the people
   Zealots

These tables show that different tendencies crisscrossed the same party: the most hostile to the Romans, the Zealots, were also the most conservative on the nationalist plane. Jesus ended up creating unanticipated alliances against himself (Mk. 3:6; Lk. 23:12). The problems need to be re-examined.

One place to begin is with the country, which sought internal, religious, political and economic autonomy. Even the Jews of the diaspora shared in this effort.

Events abroad were always the fuses which caused explosions among groups within the country. For example:

1. threats of war by the Parthians in the northeast and the Arabs in the southeast;
2. the pressure of foreigners (Phoenicians on the coast, Greeks brought in by Herod);
3. most of all, the Roman occupation.

These explosive events revealed the power struggle among:

1. the heritage of religious power of the traditional high priests;
2. the heritage of powerful families, the "lay nobility";
3. the heritage of the Herods;
4. the scribes' power of knowledge;
5. the counter-power of the Zealots against Rome and the high priest;
6. the Roman power.

These powers were based on:

1. the traditional organization represented by the possession of property;
2. the upsurge of political powers (Herod) or ideological powers (scribes);
3. necessary co-existence with Rome.

In the first two cases, the important role of families must be noted.

1. Sources of Wealth
There were commercial transactions, an example being the money changers who could play on different rates among currencies, but wealth came primarily from the land. In the time of Christ, the trend was not to invest in livestock but in land and real property, as Judas did (Acts 1:18).

Land takes its value from the mere fact of an increase in the stock of money. It was bought by big businessmen, somtimes from Tyre and Sidon; especially in Galilee, it was bought by the priestly families in Jerusalem and by the friends of Herod. Herod the Great had stimulated the circulation of money and encouraged urbanization. People knew that they could sell agricultural products in Italy, which always needed them. Some people could give an offering of a million denarii even in times of want. Speculation was ever present.

The other side:

There were very many day-laborers, paid one denarius plus food, and these were often unemployed. In Galilee they constituted a migratory mass, inured to misery.

Artisans were better off and better thought of. There were also many petty merchants, such as water sellers.

The marginal people included: the ill, those left near the temple, beggars (though there were institutions for charity), and parasites (that is, those "forced" to participate at weddings, funerals, and pilgrimages).

2. Slaves

Slaves of Jewish origin were protected by law. They had to be well treated and could not be required to perform dishonoring actions, such as washing feet or removing shoes (Jn. 1:27; 13:5–7). Free at the end of six years, they could decide to remain with their master (Ex. 26:2–11; 22:20). Herod sold abroad brigands whom he captured in Galilee.

Slaves of foreign origin could remain in slavery for life. There were only a few of them, since they were expensive, costing two thousand denarii. Slaves were part of an inheritance, and were found especially in the great families. Among them were many Arabs captured by Herod. Often coming from Tyre, they were sold in Jerusalem. A wounded slave was set free (Ex. 21:26–27).

Note:

When reading the Gospels we are struck by the number of demons driven out by Jesus and the exorcisms which he performed. We must remember that in that splintered political situation, ordinary people suffered from a general sense of insecurity. The pressure of the social and political struggles that weighed on men inevitably resulted in a large number of neuroses and psychological disturbances, which were apparently due to the rupture of social bonds. The result was a really psychological dissolution, especially among the common people, who were incapable of establishing themselves in a better situation. In this fragile society, the humblest felt the need to have recourse to dark forces to gain protection. Along with this, we see the number of magicians increase—though they were forbidden to practice in Israel—as well as the number of itinerant healers.

A slave could become a Jew: a woman by a ritual bath, a man by circumsion, or by a ritual bath if he was already circumcised, as the Arabs were. Having become a Jew, a slave was protected by the law. He practiced the religion as the women did and took part in the Passover, but he did not enter the community unless he was freed. The few freedmen were despised (Jn. 8:33–35). A circumcised slave could not read the law in the synagogue, nor could he be sold to a pagan.

Some prices given in the Gospels:
The perfumes in Mark 14:5: 300 denarii, or 300 days' labor for a farm worker.
The debt in Matthew 10:24: 10,000 talents represented the total compensation of 150,000 employees in a modern factory in a French provincial city.
Jesus was sold for 30 shekels or 120 denarii—120 days' wages.

Chapter 16

Priests

Priests were not the kind we know. Rather, they were from a single blood line, with a strict hierarchy, and their duty was to offer sacrifice in the temple.

1. A Group of the Same Blood

The priesthood was hereditary. Only the descendants of Aaron, Moses' brother, could be priests. As a result, the hereditary line was carefully safeguarded, and marriages were rigidly regulated. A priest had to marry a woman as pure as himself, so her genealogy was scrutinized, and every priest's genealogy was kept in the archives. The wife could be the daughter of a priest in office, of a Levite or of an unblemished Israelite. If she was a widow, she had to be the widow of a priest. A priest could not marry a woman who had been a prisoner or even one who had lived in an occupied city, much less a foreigner.

The result of this jealous supervision of blood purity was that if a priest contracted even a doubtful marriage, he would be declared profane and hence he and his sons would be excluded from the priesthood. After every political disturbance the priestly genealogies were scrupulously redrawn.

At the age of twenty, the son of a priest was presented at the temple, where he had to prove the legitimacy of his birth. The fact that he had no physical defect was also verified. Then he was ordained by a purifying bath and clothed with sacred habits (linen pantaloons, an alb, a cincture, a turban), and a series of sacrifices were offered. The whole process took a week.

At the most, priests constituted a group of 8,400, and there were 9,600 Levites. With wives and children the group came to 20,000 or 25,000 people. However a figure of 7,500 priests would be a safer estimate.

2. Their Life

a. Temple service

Priests were divided into twenty-four classes. Each class had responsibility for the service for one week, with rotating roles, under the orders of the head of the class. Priests drew lots for their duties for each week (Lk. 1:8–9). Classes were divided into sections, one for each day of the week, and each section had its head. A priest went to Jerusalem for two weeks annually in addition to the three great pilgrimages. At the temple the priests took charge of the sacrifices, inspected the animals, offered the sacrifices and, finally, sold the hides. They lived on their share of the meat offered in sacrifice. As a result of eating a great deal of meat, drinking water and walking barefoot in the temple, priests were often ill, and there was no doctor in the temple.

63

b. *Outside the temple*

About 1,500 priests lived in Jerusalem. The rest were in the country, especially in Judea. (Bethphage was a village of priests.) They lived on tithes (when the peasants paid them) and declared individuals to have leprosy or to be cured of it, in which case the cured person had to go to the temple. The priests in Jerusalem were fairly rich, but sometimes they were quite poor elsewhere. Many carried on a trade. Herod, for example, hired 1,800 priests for the temple as stonecutters and carpenters. Some were even in business. The majority were scribes: they explained the law, spoke in the synagogues (though this was not obligatory), sat on tribunals and counseled the people. Some were educated men, but others were not.

After the return from exile in 530 B.C., since the descendants of David had been dispossessed by the Persians, the priests assumed power and kept it until Herod. In reality, only a few great families exercised it.

3. *Hierarchy*

The high priest, then:

| (a) Priest commander of the temple, second to the high priest, the "sagan." He regulated ceremonies and policed the temple. | (b) 24 heads of weekly classes ⬇ and 156 heads of daily sections. | (c) 7 priest-overseers of the temple. Kept the temple keys. ⬇ 4 chief Levites ⬇ and guards. | (d) 3 priest treasurers in charge of the sale of animals and cult objects. (A day of pilgrimage required 93 priests.) ⬇ Manager of the temple revenues. | (e) Chief of the Levites. ⬇ 2 sections: singers and musicians; servants. |

Chapter 17

The High Priest

After the return from Babylon the high priest, a direct descendant of Zadok, Solomon's high priest, exercised all power in Palestine in God's name, at least theoretically. The Romans and later Herod acted to restrict his powers, yet the memory of the glorious past fed the desire to regain that former influence. The other powers suspected this, as the following example shows.

From the first century B.C. the high priest was not consecrated by anointing with oil, but by investiture, the handing over of garments. To obtain the high priests' submission, Herod, Archelaus and the Romans declared themselves "guardians" of the sacred garments and kept them in the Antonia tower, only lending them for feasts. This was a great vexation. In 45, the Emperor Claudius returned them to the Jews through his intermediary, Herod Agrippa II.

1. Functions

a. The high priest was the head of the Jews in Palestine and abroad. Even when Rome, and then Herod, assumed the political power, he remained the head of the national cult, head of the priests, chief official of the temple, manager of the temple's properties and president of the Sanhedrin.

b. He took part in the sacrifices whenever he wished, but always on the great feasts. In particular, he presided over worship during the week preceding the Feast of the Atonement. On that day he was the only one in the whole year who went into the Holy of Holies to ask pardon of God for the people's sins, and he slept in the temple all that week.

Even greater purity was exacted of him than of priests. Not only could he not touch a dead body, like the priests, but he could not even touch anything which had belonged to a deceased person, including anything from his own family. If he was in a state of impurity, the high priest could not function in the temple; his assistant, the commander of the temple,

---

The illegitimate high priests

Three things rendered high priests "illegitimate" in the first century B.C. and caused them to be rejected by the Essenes and some Pharisees:

1. In 175 B.C. an unworthy priest, Jason, replaced his brother Onias II, and disorders broke out over the succession. One family, the Hasmoneans, seized power. They were ordinary priests, not descendants of Zadok.

2. The mother of John Hyrcanus, high priest from 134 to 104, had been a prisoner of war, and her integrity was therefore suspect.

3. From 37 B.C. Herod or the Romans appointed whomever they wished.

then replaced him. If this was for the Feast of the Atonement, the assistant was counted among the high priests.

On the death of a high priest, debts were remitted and involuntary homicides were pardoned.

2. *His Position*

After 37 B.C. the situation changed, for Herod abolished the lifelong, hereditary sovereign pontificate in order to appoint an unknown as high priest, a descendant of Zadok living in Babylon. He did this to eliminate the family of the traditional high priests. Later Herod and the procurators appointed any priest they wished to the post. From 37 B.C. to 70 A.D. there were twenty-eight high priests, twenty-five of whom came from the ranks of ordinary priests. Thus a sacerdotal aristocracy was built up, consisting of the survivors of the legitimate family (though a good part of the Zadok line had taken refuge in Egypt from the second century B.C.) and members of the families of those who became high priests. Actually, the deposed high priests remained influential—Annas, for example, when his son-in-law Caiaphas held the power. These families, called the "high priests" in the Gospels, were rivals in influence for the post.

Four families furnished twenty-two high priests, as follows:
the Boethos family: eight;
the family of Annas: also eight;
the Phali and Kamith, three each.

Since a high priest could have but one wife, the daughter of a priest, Levite or "true Israelite," he married his betrothed as young as possible (twelve and a half), seeking fruitful alliances. Such favors made it possible for him to place relatives in good positions, that is, to practice nepotism.

Caught between the demands of the Pharisees and those of Herod or the Roman powers, high priests espoused a prudent conservatism (Jn. 11:48—49).

Here is a first-century complaint about their grasping for power:
Unhappy am I because of the family of Boethos;
   Unhappy am I because of their spear.
Unhappy am I because of the family of Annas;
   Unhappy am I because of their talk.
Unhappy am I because of the family of Phali;
   Unhappy am I because of their fists.
For they are high priests, their sons are treasurers,
   their sons-in-law are temple overseers;
And their servants beat the people with sticks.

Chapter 18

Procurator
(Roman prefect)

To understand the role of the procurator, we must recall how Rome organized its empire. While leaving conquered peoples their laws and customs, Rome was represented by high-ranking agents. From the table below, we can see the differences at the time of Christ.

1. Italy and colonies of former soldiers and free cities	2. Countries linked by treaty	3. Egypt	4. Other territories belonged to the Roman people who had conquered them by arms; all inhabitants paid tribute	
(The number of free cities constantly increased)	Retained internal autonomy	Personal property of the emperor	(a) Senatorial provinces	(b) Imperial provinces
Inhabitants were Roman citizens	Their king was an "ally of the Roman people" (cf. Herod)	Administered by a prefect	Conquered before the empire (29 B.C.)	Occupied by the legions
Exempted from paying tribute; could participate in choice of magistrates			Under the Roman senate	Directed by a senator
			Directed by a governor with the rank of senator (proconsul); it was a good end to a career	Appppointed and dismissed by the emperor; senator was assisted by a prefect, chief of legions and a civilian chief, the procurator, in charge of finances
Fell under Roman courts (cf. Paul); could not be subjected to degrading penalties, like the cross			Later the emperor sent chevalier procurators to see to his interests; they levied some taxes	Augustus reorganized the administration; all provinces ended by depending on the emperor
Their rights were hereditary				For a small territory or one difficult to administer, the emperor appointed a chevalier prefect to handle everything: this prefect (e.g., Pilate) was called procurator under Claudius

The Roman prefect, then procurator, in Judea and later in Palestine was under the Roman legate in Syria but kept considerable autonomy. He resided in Caesarea or, for feasts, in Jerusalem, living in the royal palace or the Antonia tower. He let the Sanhedrin exercise justice but reserved the death penalty for himself. He levied the Roman taxes.

He had a rather small force of about three thousand soldiers. There was a garrison with a cohort and a tribune at Jerusalem, augmented during feasts, and another at Acco, i.e., Ptolemais. There were Roman posts in the fortresses built by Herod at Cypres, near Jericho, Macheronte and elsewhere. The soldiers were principally Syrian or non-Jewish auxiliaries, since Jews, for religious reasons, were exempt from serving in the armies. The bulk of the troops as well as storehouses and the Roman administration remained in Caesarea.

Generally speaking the procurator respected Jewish customs, but Pilate provoked a riot by bringing the Roman standards into Jerusalem. Yet he kept close supervision and between the years 6 and 41 he named the high priest eight times.

A man had to be a chevalier by birth to obtain this position of prefect or pay 400,000 sesterces to buy the title. (To become a senator cost 1,000,000 sesterces.)

ROMAN GOVERNMENT IN PALESTINE		PROCURATOR
Dates	Emperor and Legate in Syria	Procurator in Palestine (in all Judea until 41)
6	AUGUSTUS, emperor QUIRINUS, legate for second time	Herod Archelaus removed. Hated by the Jews "even more than Herod." COPONIUS prefect of Judea. New census to fix taxes provoked riot. Revolt of Judas the Galilean.
9		MARCUS AURELIUS
12		ANNIUS RUFUS
15	TIBERIUS, emperor	VALERIUS GRATUS, deposed three high priests in three years. In 18 named Caiaphas to replace his father-in-law Annas.
17	GERMANICUS, legate adopted son of Tiberius; riot in 19	
26		PONTIUS PILATE, unpopular procurator. Emperor ordered him to take down the Roman bucklers from the royal palace in Jerusalem. Took silver from the temple to build an aqueduct, since the Sanhedrin had neglected the water problem. Indignation, riots, deaths. In Samaria, a false prophet assembled the Samaritans on Mount Garizim. Pilate massacred them.
35	VITELLIUS, legate	Dismissed Pontius Pilate. Caligula ordered exile or suicide for him (37).
36		Departure of Pilate left a void. MARCELLUS, prefect.
37	CALIGULA, emperor	MARULLUS.
39	PETRONIUS, legate	A statue of Caligula was overturned in Jamnia. The emperor ordered it to be set up in Jerusalem. The legate of Syria and Herod Agrippa let the matter lag. In January 41 Caligula was assassinated.
41	CLAUDIUS, emperor	
42	CILIUS MARSIUS, legate	HEROD AGRIPPA I, king, more than prefect. Martyrdom of James.

44		*Death of Agrippa. CUSPIUS FADUS, procurator of all Palestine, called Judea. Revolt of Theudas (Acts 5:36). Killed by the army; his head exposed in Jerusalem.*
45	**CASSIUS LONGINUS,** legate	
46		*TIBERIUS JULIUS ALEXANDER, apostate Jew. Famine (Acts 11:28). Crucified two brothers of Judas the Galilean. Later became prefect of Egypt.*
48		*VENTIDUS CURANUS. Took the part of Samaritans who had killed pilgrims going from Galilee to Jerusalem. Riots. Recalled by the legate; exiled.*
50	**QUADRATUS,** legate	
52		*ANTONINUS FELIX. Favorite of Claudius. His third marriage was to Drusilla, sister of Agrippa II. "He exercised the power of a king with the soul of a slave." Recalled by Nero. In 57, revolts (cf. Acts 21:38 re the Egyptian) to obtain equal rights at Caesarea for Jews, Greeks and Syrians.*
54	**NERO,** emperor	
59		*PROCIUS FESTUS. Restored order. Died in office. His death left a void. Martyrdom of James of Jerusalem by the high priest Annas II, grandson of Annas.*
60	**CORBULON,** legate	
62		*LUCCEIUS ALBINUS. Venal. Kidnaping of hostages by hired assassins to obtain release of prisoners.*
63	**GALLUS,** legate	
64		*GESSIUS FLORES. Disorders increased. Anarchy.*
66	**VESPASIAN,** emperor	*TITUS. Open revolt*

Chapter 19

Professions and Weights and Measures

In the first place, it must be realized that in first-century Palestine there was a hierarchy of professions, but the rank was different from ours, because there was no opposition between intellectual and manual work. The opposition was, rather, between "pure" and "impure" occupations. An occupation which touched blood or the dead was "impure"—tanning, for example. It was also considered impure or vile to be a slave or to work in the transportation of goods because of the temptation to steal or the risk of touching something dirty. Some trades were looked down upon, such as that of jeweler because it led to contacts with wealthy women.

It must also be remembered that the boundaries between occupations were sometimes blurred. A carpenter was also a mason; a spice seller in the market also cultivated a piece of land, etc. Besides those engaged in agricultural work, there were also many artisans, who were generally well regarded. A carpenter was also esteemed. In cities, workers grouped together in quarters, and some were required to do this, like tanners who had to live outside the walls.

Construction trades were known. Palestine had many stone quarries (underground, in Jerusalem). A "carpenter" was a mason, as well as a worker in wood, and quite able to build a whole house. Basalt, called "iron stone" because of its hardness, was extracted from the vicinity of the Dead Sea.

Many villages had their potters, street peddlers, weavers (especially women), and tailors. In Jerusalem, the tanners' corporation received the hides of sacrificed animals, which belonged to the priests. Palestine's woolen cloth was quite well known.

Small trading was most common. A fairly large city had a bazaar divided into quarters for each specialty, but every village also had its market.

There was even a luxury item, silver, which came from Egypt or Arabia. Palestine produced perfumes, at first for the temple and, in Herod's reign, for export.

Large cities had doctors, barbers, and street cleaners. Jerusalem had a drainage ditch, two meters deep and eighty centimeters wide.

A note on shepherds: they were inclined to theft and would mark one sheep out of ten for themselves. The number of shepherds decreased as the rich preferred to invest in land, which made a surer return.

There was great fear of unemployment in Palestine. The trades were organized into associations to insure respect for hours of work and regularity of pay.

Weights

A talent equaled 75.4 lbs.; a mina, .02 oz. Used also as money.

One shekel equaled 4 oz. To distinguish the coin from the weight, it was called a silver shekel.

There was also a pound (11½ oz.) brought from Rome.

Measures

In principle, measuring began with the human body (foot, forearm, pace). Large differences developed and each measure had to be designated by country: a Roman pace.

A mile in Rome was	in Syria,	in Palestine,
4,881 ft.	5,191 ft.	5,074 ft.
or 7.5 stadia of 650 ft.	692 ft.	677 ft.
or 750 spans of 6.5 ft.	6.9 ft.	6.7 ft.
or 1,500 paces of 3.3 ft.	3.5 ft.	3.38 ft.
or 3,000 cubits of 1.65 ft.	1.75 ft.	1.69 ft.
or 4,500 feet of 1.1 ft.	1.2 ft.	1.13 ft.

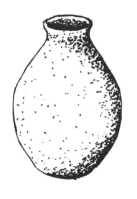

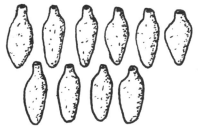

One kor held between 92 and 112 gallons. In the time of Christ, 112 gallons (450 liters) equaled ten jars holding 9 to 11 gallons of liquids.

For grain, a kor of between 91 and 112 gallons was divided into 10 epha or into 41 bushels which measured 2.2 gallons (8.75 liters) each.

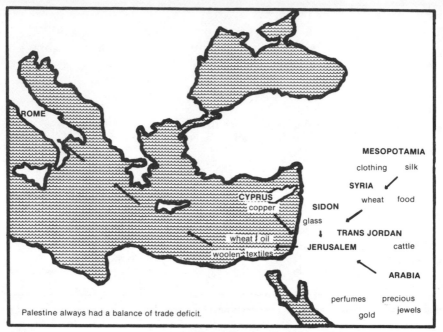

Palestine always had a balance of trade deficit.

FOREIGN COMMERCE OF PALESTINE

Chapter 20

Proselytes

The word "proselyte" comes from a Greek word meaning "to draw near."

1. The Opening Out of Judaism

Judaism was linked to a people. Little by little this people discovered the universality of God, especially after the trial of the Babylonian exile. Reflection by the prophets and sages led to their proposing the law of Moses as an ideal which should be proclaimed to the world.

Then there began a time of Jewish missions to present Judaism to other cultures (Mt. 23:15), and Jewish missionaries traveled over the known world. Even in cities far distant from Palestine, Jews propagated their faith.

"The pagan has no father." This proverb underscores the idea that, since he was not a "son of Abraham" by birth, the pagan had no genealogy to place him among the chosen people. He could only rely on his own efforts to find the truth. At the beginning, he was thought to be immoral, but upon conversion, he was considered to be a new person. It was a birth.

2. Conversion of Pagans

Conversion had two stages:

a. The pagan learned the law and began to respect certain rules of Israelite religious behavior—not to eat blood, for example, and to keep the sabbath. He was then called a proselyte at the door, for he was at the entrance to the Jewish religion.

b. Then he was admitted as an affiliate of the Jewish faith; he obviously could not become Jewish by blood. He was next circumcised unless he was a hemophiliac, plunged in a ritual bath, and allowed to offer sacrifices. Then, as a "proselyte of justice," he participated in the Passover and other Jewish feasts.

From that point on, he was subject to all the prescriptions of the Jewish law. This was a real rupture with his former life. Bonds that he had contracted, even marriage, were considered non-existent, and he had to remake such bonds as he completely adopted the Jewish style of life.

Nevertheless, the proselyte of justice did not have all the rights of the born Jew. He could not sit on the Sanhedrin, nor on a court judging persons, but he could sit on a court deciding on property. Nor could his daughter marry a priest. Certain conditions barred him from obtaining official posts. He could, however, receive assistance from the second tithe if he was in want.

Where Did the Pagans Come From?

From almost everywhere: there were a great number near Jewish communities in foreign countries, and many were from places near Palestine, such as Auran and Idumea. Herod's family were proselytes.

There were more women than men proselytes, since circumcision was considered degrading by pagans.

Abroad, the proselytes were characterized by a cult which rejected images of God and obeyed strict moral rules. Synagogues were open to all who believed in the one God of Israel. This was true even in Jerusalem, where there were synagogues for proselytes.

Those Who Fear God

This term comes from the respect with which the Bible surrounds the law and the worship of God. "The fear of God is the beginning of wisdom." This expression designated the pagans who embraced the monotheistic faith, the one God of Israel, without fulfilling all the practices and without being circumcised. The expression was sometimes synonymous with the proselyte at the door.

Texts concerning proselytes
(The baptism mentioned is the ritual bath)
Rabbi Eleazar says: The proselyte circumcised and not baptized is a true proselyte, for we find that our fathers were circumcised but not baptized. Rabbi Josue accepts the same doctrine by taking the example of mothers, who were baptized but not circumcized. The sages required both baptism and circumcision. All agree on the necessity of circumcision, but not of baptism.

Tradition of the rabbis: A proselyte must be informed that he is about to become a proselyte at a time when Israel's situation is one of persecution. Then, if he says he knows that, he should be instructed in the commandments, both the light and the grave, and the punishments entailed by their violation. He must also be instructed in the rewards of fidelity reserved for Israel the just in future times. He will be circumcised. Once healed, he will be baptized with two rabbis instructing him in the commandments. Then he is like an Israelite in all regards. For a woman, two rabbis will instruct her, remaining outside the bath.

Rabbi José: Proselytes who become such are like newborn infants. They are in pain because they are not skilled in keeping the commandments like the Israelites, or because they act out of fear and not love.

Chapter 21

Publicans

The word "publican" comes from the Latin *publicanus*, which means having to do with the public domain. The publican was occupied with one aspect of public life: taxes. He operated on two levels:

a. That of "general farmer," a man who farms taxes, that is, he paid Rome either the direct taxes or the total amount of the indirect levies and taxes due from a city or district, an amount which was fixed by Rome. He then reimbursed himself from the people by whatever means he thought best. As very great sums of money were involved, he also played the role of banker.

b. That of local collector in the service of a local prince, a much more humble level than the above. The term was applied to the employees of general farmers or those charged with collecting taxes, *octrois* (a tax on commodities), or tolls for the king or, through the intermediary of his chiefs, for Rome.

Usually in both cases the man who conducted the collection of taxes received a five-year lease. He was free as to the means by which he reimbursed himself. There were associations of publicans.

Clearly, very great abuses occurred, and the general farmers became quite rich. To prevent truly extravagant abuses, the chief publicans were gradually replaced, during the course of the first century, by local magistrates who oversaw municipalities and took care of direct taxes. Farming continued for indirect taxes but such rights were leased in smaller blocs.

Considering that the only just tax concerned the temple and, by extension, the people of Israel, the Jews regarded the collection of taxes for Rome as collaboration with the enemy, treason against the people and a religious insult to God, the sole king of Israel. Although some Palestinian circles were less strict with regard to taxes paid to Rome, public opinion in general held publicans in contempt and many refused to have any but obligatory contact with them. Publicans were outside the pale, stripped of their civil rights, and could not be judges or even witnesses at trials. It was forbidden to change money with them.

The Gospels speak only of publicans of the second rank. Christ went to their homes and thus broke down the wall of contempt around them.

Levi (Matthew) worked in Capernaum near the port; therefore he worked for Herod Antipas. Zacchaeus, at Jericho, probably controlled the balm trade and worked for the Roman prefect.

Chapter 22

Ritual Purity

In the Gospels, we often see allusions to what is pure and impure, to the Jews' ablutions, etc. Purity had a much wider connotation than sexual purity. It concerned the whole of man's conduct and his connection with the objects which surrounded him, and expressed one's integrity in body and mind.

1. Origin

Classifications into "pure" and "impure" are very ancient and they exist in all religions. They are not exactly the same as sacred and profane. Taking only objects, the following definitions might give an idea.

The part of the world which man masters, organizes and commands is *profane.*

The whole of the obscure forces which rule the world and escape man's control are *sacred.* The sacred frightens but also attracts, for if man is able to conciliate it, it can be beneficent.

The pure is that which makes man capable of approaching the sacred: the places, objects, times which prepare for approach to the sacred. Moses took off his shoes in order to draw near to the holy place of the burning bush (Ex. 3:5). One must be righteous to approach the sacred.

"For I am the Lord your God; consecrate yourselves therefore and be holy, for I am holy. For I am the Lord who brought you up out of the land of Egypt to be your God; you shall therefore be holy, for I am holy" (Lev. 11:44–45).
Jesus' position:
"There is nothing outside a man which, by going into him, can defile him; but the things which come out of a man are what can defile him. . . . (Thus he declared all foods clean)" (Mk. 7:23).
See also Acts 10:18 ("I should not call any man unclean") and Romans 14–15.

The impure is whatever distances man from the sacred. In a word, whatever diminishes the vital energy is impure, such as sickness, death, animals whose flesh it is dangerous to eat, or any sexual flow. The impure is contagious; it spreads when touched. When a priest touched a corpse, he became impure.

2. *Ritual Purity*

The prophets spoke most often of purity of heart, but Jewish customs highly esteemed the obligatory gestures to insure purity for approaching God, prayer, and the temple.

Among these codified actions or rites were ablutions with prayer by which man effaced impure contacts. The pious Jew made seven such a day:

1. On rising, he washed his hands, face, and mouth. If he had had a nightmare, he took a bath.
2. Before meals (recommended).
3. After meals (required).
4, 5, 6. Before the three daily prayers ("Hear, O Israel").
7. Before going to bed.

One whole book, Leviticus, explains the rules of purity.

What is impure

Blood *and whatever it touches, for it is life. To pour out blood is to pour out life.*

Sex, *for it consumes vital energy.*

Death *and everything relating to it.*

Sickness, *especially leprosy.*

What is impure

Animals *which do not graze or have cloven hoofs.*

Birds, *predators, night birds.*

Reptiles *all; they crawl.*

Fish *without scales or fins.*

Pagans, *their idols, and their countries.*

Chapter 23

The Romans

At the time of Christ, Rome was headed by a successful military leader, the emperor, who had taken over the political government. The Roman senate had lost its powers. The emperor commanded 350,000 soldiers. He oversaw the governors of the provinces and, desiring to keep them from growing rich too quickly, provided a comfortable salary, about a million sesterces annually, in addition to other advantages.

In the conquered territories, Rome tried to preserve local cultures. Rome retained for itself control of foreign policy, of currency, and of roads; friendly officials were kept in these posts—often made to remain friendly because their children were being raised in Rome—and Rome received a large tribute and exacted the provision of foods. Thus, Rome managed to control a country with a minimum of troops. The imperial cult of the emperor as "august," that is, divine, had a unifying role. Mercenaries were recruited in the area. For religious reasons, Jews were not enrolled in the army nor did they honor the imperial cult, but they offered sacrifices to God for the emperor.

In the East, the legate of Syria, who resided in Syria at Antioch, was both military head, assisted by a chief of legions, and civil governor, assisted by a procurator for financial matters. He commanded up to three legions, each of which had its workshops and depots.

In Palestine, the prefect, later procurator, commanded about three thousand soldiers, whose duty was to maintain order and defend the frontiers: in the east against the Persians, in the south against the brigands. Five cohorts of foot soldiers and five hundred mounted men divided the duty. There were few Romans among these troops; they were mainly Syrians, Samaritans and other mercenaries.

The right of Roman citizenship was granted after twenty years of service as a legionnaire and twenty-five as an auxiliary. The new citizen adopted Roman customs and law. Former soldiers were settled in colonies, towns and territories which they peopled, cultivated and organized. This title could be bought (Acts 22:25–28) or granted to the inhabitants of a city. The right could be lost through conviction by a court.

LEGION	commanded by a legate	consisted of six cohorts of 6,000 to 10,000 men
COHORT	a tribune	six centuries of 600 to 1000 men
CENTURY	a centurion	60 to 100 men

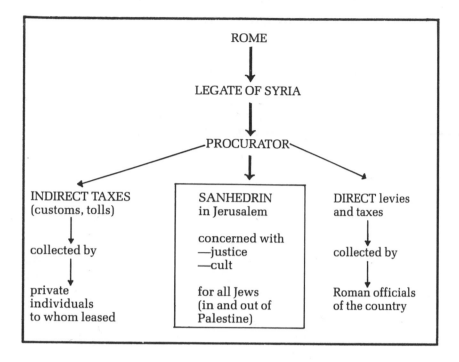

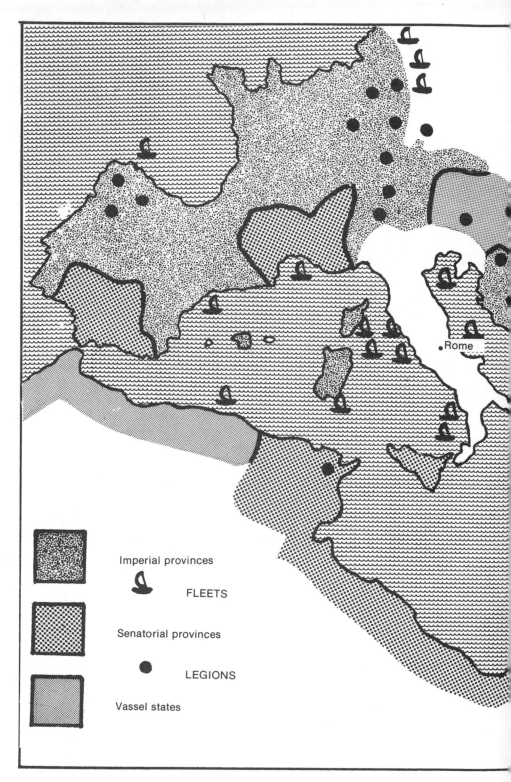

Imperial provinces

FLEETS

Senatorial provinces

LEGIONS

Vassel states

Rome

THE ROMAN EMPIRE AT THE TIME OF CHRIST

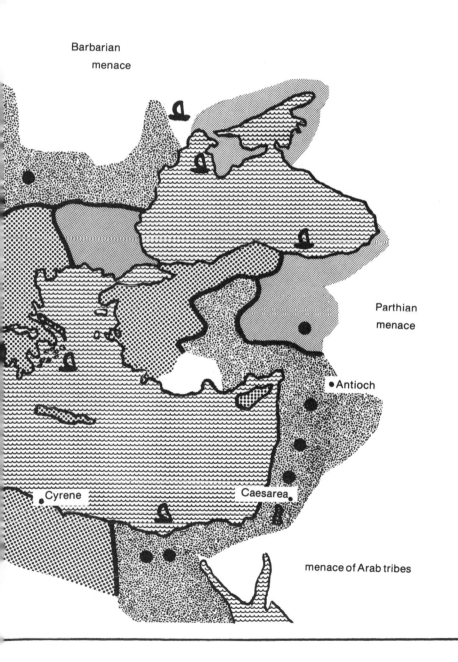

Barbarian menace

Parthian menace

Antioch

Cyrene

Caesarea

menace of Arab tribes

Chapter 24

The Sabbath

The word "sabbath" comes, perhaps, from a verb meaning to stop, to rest. It designated the day extending from Friday evening to Saturday evening, for a day ran from one sunset to the next. It was the only day of the week to have a name, all others being indicated by numbers.

Originally the weekly day of rest seems to have been connected with the four phases of the moon, since the calendar, as was mentioned, was a lunar calendar. In Mesopotamia these four days were ill-omened, and hence not working days. It appears that in Canaan, the sabbath was the feast of the full moon, a holiday from whatever agricultural work was in season. These later became weekly feasts.

These days recalled the three origins: first the departure from Egypt, then the Sinai covenant, and then, moving back in time, the creation of the world.

By this means, Israel absorbed a very ancient substratum into its history, its law and its religion. The division of time into seven days seems to have come from an ancient people, the Sumerians, who were in Mesopotamia by the sixth millennium, and whose system of counting had seven as its base.

Because of the inability to go to the temple at Jerusalem, observance of the sabbath was intensified after the Babylonian exile and with the Maccabean revolt in the middle of the second century B.C. (Read, for example, 1 Macc. 2:32–38.) According to Isaiah (58:13–14) the sabbath was a festival day, a day of delights.

The Sabbath Day

The sabbath was a feast day, a day for prayer and meditation on the Scriptures, especially the law of Moses.

On Friday evening, in the villages, the chief of the synagogue would announce the beginning of the sabbath by sounding three trumpet blasts. Work stopped and shops were closed. Rabbis taught that twenty-nine activities were forbidden on the sabbath—for example, commerce, manual labor, lighting a fire, and cooking. No one could travel more than "a sabbath day's journey" (¼ to ¾ mile). In every house, the wife lighted an oil lamp, and thus symbolized the opposite of Eve who, by sinning, had extinguished light. Also, the wife was the mistress of the house. Everyone dressed appropriately.

The cooking was done in advance for the evening meal, and guests were invited. The Pharisees often took this meal together. Two special loaves were baked and, as a sign of a feast, a cup of wine was shared.

On Saturday morning people went to the synagogue to hear the law and to pray. In Jerusalem they went to the temple for a solemn liturgy. After the noon meal, one could go to the "house of study" near the synagogue to listen to the rabbis' discussions. Dinner was the ritual repast.

A trumpet blast at nightfall announced the end of the sabbath. The day of joy, prayer and quiet ended with a prayer.

Jesus and the Sabbath

The best of the rabbis had written: "You can save a life on the sabbath because the sabbath was given to you; you were not given over to the sabbath." Christ placed himself in this perspective and enlarged it: "The sabbath was made for man and not man for the sabbath" (Mk. 2:27). He insisted on the obligation of doing good, of fraternal love, for he was master of the sabbath, and the cures he performed on that day were an invitation to works of charity. In rising against the strict conventions of the sabbath (Mt. 12:2–8; Lk. 13:14–17) Christ did not eliminate it but respected it (Lk 4:16) and made of it a day for sharing in love.

The Bible gives three origins of the sabbath:
1. To recall the deliverance from Egypt:
"You shall remember that you were a servant in the land of Egypt and that the Lord your God brought you out thence with a mighty hand and an outstretched arm: therefore the Lord your God commanded you to keep the sabbath day."

Dt. 5:15.

2. To recall God's resting after the creation:
"In six days the Lord made heaven and earth, the sea and all that is in them, and rested (did not work) the seventh day; therefore the Lord blessed the seventh day and hallowed it."

Ex. 20:11

3. To recall the gift of the covenant:
"Therefore the people of Israel will keep the sabbath, observing the sabbath throughout their generations as a perpetual covenant. It is a sign forever between me and the people of Israel."

Ex. 31:16–17

Ancient peoples held that each month had ill-omened days during which it was forbidden by the gods to work and to travel. For the Assyrians, the 1st, 7th, 14th, 19th, 24th, and 28th days were considered dangerous. The week of seven days divided the nomads' lunar calendar of twenty-eight days into four weeks.

Chapter 25

Sacrifices

1. Definitions

The origin, nature and role of sacrifices have been lost in the mist of time. The notion of sacrifice varied according to the social organization and the situation of the human group. It either stressed the communication of vital energy, as in farming societies, for example, or submission to God in very hierarchical societies. But in every case there was a bond, a relationship between the world of God and the world of man, and this involved drawing on the life which eluded man.

Sacrifices usually had two opposing poles: to deprive oneself and to offer. From this opposition, several solutions were possible.

A. *Man deprives himself and offers to God.*
    God is recognized as master; he is appeased.
    Violence is averted; man lives.
    Purpose: appeasement.
    Biblical type: peace offering.

B. *By depriving himself, man gains God's favor.*
    By means of what he offers, man puts himself in an advantageous situation vis-à-vis God. In return, God hears him.
    Purpose: exchange.
    Biblical type: sacrifices.

C. *By making an offering, man opens himself to the sacred.*
    The sacred, the divine, is everywhere present in a diffused way. By depriving himself, man opens himself to the presence of the sacred which becomes concentrated at this point.
    Purpose: presence.
    Biblical type: holocaust.

D. *By offering, man frees himself.*
    Man frees himself from the rights of the sacred which has mastery over life. Thus, having offered something, man is master of the rest.
    Purpose: compensation.
    Biblical type: first fruits.

2. The Bible

The preceding outline provides a general description, for the types of sacrifice became mixed during the course of time: the smoke of burning victims rose as a perfume to appease God. The people of the Bible took over the rites of the people who had lived before them. Thus, the patriarchs offered a sacrifice where God had manifested himself (Gen. 8:20;

12:7, 13, 18, etc.), and the worship which had been offered in a number of places (Shechem, Shiloh, Beersheba, etc.) was later centered in the temple at Jerusalem (Dt. 12).

There were various kinds of sacrifices, as described in the Book of Leviticus:

a. **Holocaust:** from the Greek words *holo*, meaning entire, and *kaio*, to burn—to burn a victim entirely on the altar.

b. **Peace offering:** blood was poured out on the altar, the fat (where life was stored) was burned, and the flesh was divided between the priest and the men making the offering.

c. **Vegetable offering:** bread, oil, wine, offered or poured out. A special perfume with an incense base was also burned on the altar of perfumes in the "holy" of the temple.

d. **First fruits:** an offering of a portion of a first crop or a first-born male.

These sacrifices took place every day, morning and evening, on sabbaths and feast days. They were offered by individuals, by groups, by notables.

3. At the Time of Christ

In the rebuilt temple, care was taken that the liturgy was in accord with the traditional prescriptions. Morning and evening the priests offered the holocaust of a lamb, the "perpetual sacrifice." The priests took turns celebrating in the presence of delegations of laymen who stood in the court reserved for them. On sabbaths and feast days, the number of the sacrifices that were offered increased enormously. On the completion of the temple, three hundred head of cattle were killed. Sacrifices were public in the evening. During Passover week, tens of thousands of animals were sacrificed (cattle, lambs, goats, pigeons, etc.).

The animals had to be young—one year for those offered as first fruits—and without any defect. Priests retained the right to sell them in the temple, and payment was made with a special coin: a "sanctuary

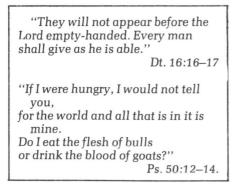

"They will not appear before the
Lord empty-handed. Every man
shall give as he is able."
Dt. 16:16–17

"If I were hungry, I would not tell
  you,
for the world and all that is in it is
  mine.
Do I eat the flesh of bulls
or drink the blood of goats?"
Ps. 50:12–14.

shekel." Money changers made the exchange. The hide went to the priest who performed the sacrifice; a first-class sheepskin cost more than sixteen denarii, or sixteen days' work for a farm laborer. It is estimated that with such a hide a priest could pay his week's lodging for his obligatory stay in the temple.

Beginning with Emperor Augustus, two sacrifices were offered for the emperor and the empire at the expense of the Roman treasury. These sacrifices were stopped at the time of the revolt in 66. Every pilgrim was required to pay a minimum of one-half a denarius, or a half day's work; the poorest offered two turtle doves (Lk. 2:24).

"If the offering is a burnt offering from the herd, he shall offer a male without blemish; he shall offer it at the door of the tent of meeting, that he may be accepted before the Lord; he shall lay his hand upon the head of the burnt offering and it shall be accepted for him to make atonement for him. Then he shall kill the bull before the Lord, and Aaron's sons the priests shall present the blood, and throw the blood round about, against the altar that is at the door of the tent of meeting. And he shall flay the burnt offering and cut it into pieces; and the sons of Aaron the priest shall put fire on the altar and lay wood in order upon the fire; and Aaron's sons the priests shall lay the pieces, the head and the fat in order upon the wood that is on the fire upon the altar, but its entrails and its legs he shall wash with water. And the priest shall burn the whole upon the altar as a burnt offering, an offering by fire, a pleasing odor to the Lord."

Lev. 1:3–9

Chapter 26

Sadducees

1. Origin

In the Sadducees' opinion, their name came from Zadok, a priest connected with the history of David and Solomon, particularly in the troubled times preceding the reign of David and the difficulties about his succession.

Before Jerusalem was taken by David, the principal sanctuaries were in Shiloh. The sons of Eli, the priest at Shiloh, had acted unjustly and had died (1 Sam. 2:12–25). Eli's descendant supported David (1 Sam. 21) who took him with himself to Jerusalem. He added another priest, Zadok, whose origin is obscure (perhaps already a member of the local clergy at Jerusalem). At the time of the succession, the first, Abiathar, took the side of David's son, Adonijah; the second, Zadok, took the part of Solomon and Bathsheba. When Solomon became king, he eliminated those who had not supported him.

Among Solomon's reforms, worship became centralized at the one temple in Jerusalem. Zadok's family thus established itself in the line of Aaron, and he alone kept the hereditary function of high priest with a stable line of descent, similar to the king's: "I will raise up for myself a faithful priest, who shall do according to what is in my heart and in my mind, and I will build him a sure house" (1 Sam. 2:35).

"It is the opinion of the Sadducees that the soul dies with the body, that the only thing we are obliged to do is to observe the law and that it is an act of virtue not to yield in wisdom to those who teach it to us. Those of this sect are but few in number, but it is composed of persons of the highest rank. Almost nothing is done except on their advice. This comes from the fact that when, against their wishes, they are elevated to posts and honors, they are constrained to conform to the conduct of the Pharisees because the people will not suffer them to do otherwise."

Flavius Josephus, Jewish Antiquities, 18, 2.

2. History

These complicated beginnings connected with royal politics were not to grow simpler. Zadok's descendants declared themselves legitimate priests at the time of the exile and at the restoration following it. Further, when Jerusalem was taken, and in the confusion of the exile, new priests appeared who claimed descent from Zadok. Hence the concern about genealogies at the return from exile, though it was never possible to eliminate the intruders.

In the second century B.C., in the period of the Maccabean revolt, the history of which had great influence at the time of Christ, the position of high priest had become a political force which the Syrian kings named Antiochus wished to control. Families were divided between those who accepted the foreign power and those who rejected it, and a general war shook the people. When the priestly family of the Maccabees (the Hasmoneans) took power in 142 B.C., they were surrounded by an aristocratic group of priests and laymen who defended the national independence and the traditions.

This group, whose ranking members were priests, thenceforth called "sons of Zadok," acted as a group from the second century on; they intervened in political life, in the entourage of the high priest who was the national leader, and in the Sanhedrin. The term Sadducees in the end meant a party recruited from the priestly class and the lay nobility.

3. Political Position

The Sadducees had three characteristics:

1. They were strongly conservative, attached to the temple and to the ancient traditions. They supported a nationalist policy until the arrival of the Romans in 63 B.C. Herod treated them with disdain. Although they were jealous of Herod, they were also rigidly opposed to the Pharisees. Herod lessened their power but covered them with honors, and they became cultic functionaries.

2. They made an effort to preserve power. Skillful tacticians, they knew how to open national affairs to outside influence. They proved accepting of Greek culture, its trade and business relationships, and were conciliatory toward the Romans, except when Pilate took the temple's gold. In short, they were open within the logic of their conservatism.

3. They were cut off from the people. However, though few in number, they were very powerful.

4. Doctrine

The Sadducees were the conservatives. They espoused fidelity to the written words of Scripture against the oral, and therefore open, tradition of the Pharisees. They considered priests to be the only authentic interpreters of the law, and they objected to laymen interpreting it—and Pharisees were laymen. They accordingly rejected any development of doctrine, such as the immortality of the soul, retribution in a future world and the resurrection (Mt. 22:23; Acts 23:8), defending a sort of vegetative life after death, "sheol." This stance constituted, in fact, a special tradition which denied the obligatory force of anything not directly written; tradition did not have the force of law. The Sadducees applied a strict moral code. There were Sadducee scribes.

Skeptical with regard to the popular messianic ideas which threatened to disturb order (Jn. 11:45–53), the Sadducees seem to have been responsible for the death of Jesus, whom they took for a political messiah (Jn. 19:15).

David's priests:

"And Zadok and Abiathar were priests and Ira the Jairite was also David's priest."

2 Sam. 20:25–26

Solomon's priests:

"So Solomon sat upon the throne of David his father and his kingdom was firmly established. . . . And to Abiathar the priest the king said, 'Go to Anathoth, to your estate, for you deserve death. But I will not at this time put you to death because you bore the ark of the Lord God before David my father and because you shared in all the afflictions of my father.' So Solomon expelled Abiathar from being priest of the Lord . . . and the king put Zadok the priest in the place of Abiathar."

1 Kgs. 2:12, 26–27, 35

Chapter 27

The Samaritans

The history of the Samaritans is complex and enigmatic. To have some understanding of it, we must remember:

1. The Palestinian tribes were unified only by David and Solomon. The fragile alliance between the North and the South crumbled in 933 B.C. on the death of Solomon.

2. While preserving traces of the separatism of the North and South, the Bible relates an effort at unity; the genealogies manifest the alliances.

1. History

When the tribes from the South were liberated by Moses and they returned from Egypt about 1250 B.C., they found Palestine inhabited by tribes which had not gone to Egypt (those of the North), or which had been expelled from Egypt in 1550 (those of the Center).

The Center of Palestine, a mountainous and wooded country, was separated from both North and South by two series of fortresses. The inhabitants, grouped in independent cities, lived by pillage and by hiring themselves out as mercenaries. When the plain of Esdralon, or Yzreel, was cultivated, the land was redistributed. In the end, a tribe established in the Center on Mount Ephraim supplanted the others. A group was formed attached to a patriarch, "Israel," which would later join with the patriarch Jacob from the South. Hence the name kingdom of Israel given to the North in distinction to kingdom of Judah (the name of the dominant tribe) in the South. The great sanctuaries, Shiloh, Shechem, etc., gathered in the people of the North. Samaria was the first of twelve districts set up by Solomon.

David and Solomon unified the country, but the northern tribes revolted against Jerusalem's excessive centralization. Toward the end of Solomon's reign (1 Kgs. 11:26–41), Jeroboam had to take refuge in Egypt, but he returned after Solomon's death and founded the northern kingdom (1 Kgs. 12).

Jeroboam established himself in Shechem, the old capital of central Palestine (Jgs. 9). To prevent pilgrimages to Jerusalem, he restored to honor the celebrated places of worship, Bethel in the south of his kingdom and Dan in the north.

The actual city of Samaria was founded about 880 B.C. by Omri (1 Kgs. 16:41). A pagan cult took root there when an alliance was formed with the important ports of Sidon and Tyre.

In constant rivalry with Damascus, Samaria was taken by Sargon II in 722, and this was the end of the kingdom of the North subject to Assyria. Huge numbers of people were deported—22,290 according to one inscription. To replace the Israelites, the governing power installed Chaldeans, Syrians, Persians, and Arabs (2 Kgs. 17:24–41). Corresponding to the mixture of nationalities was a religious mélange. Samaria was the chief city of the province for the Assyrians, then the Persians; the province was called Akrabatene.

"All Israel said:
'What portion have we in David?
We have no inheritance in the son of Jesse.
To your tents, O Israel!
Look now to your house, David!' "
1 Kgs. 12:16

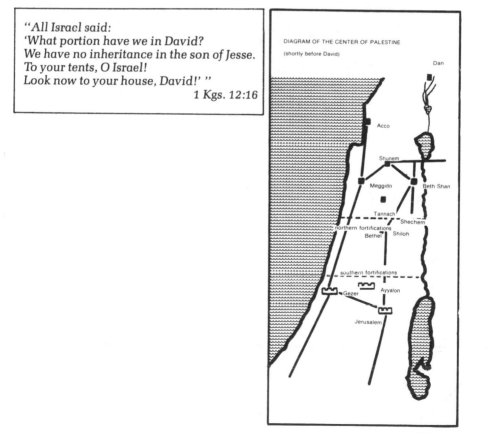

DIAGRAM OF THE CENTER OF PALESTINE
(shortly before David)

When the people from the kingdom of the South returned from exile, Samaria opposed their settling (Neh. 3:34). During the Maccabean revolt, Samaria accepted Greek laws. Judea took revenge on its hostility by destroying Samaria in 109. Herod the Great rebuilt it in 30 B.C. and called it Sebaste in honor of the emperor, Sebaste being the Greek equivalent of Augustus. He built a temple there in honor of the imperial cult. Desiring to unify his kingdom, Herod married a Samaritan. In 6 A.D. the Samaritans defiled the temple at Jerusalem by throwing human bones into it.

Galilee, because of its different origin, its location outside the center of the country and political partitioning, was separated from Samaria in 104 B.C.

3. Beliefs

This history explains the hatred of the Jews for the Samaritans. The Jews considered them worse than pagans: "Whoever eats bread with a Samaritan eats pork." Conversion of Samaritans to Judaism was sometimes forbidden. A Jew could travel through Samaria provided he did not speak to anyone, but a good Jew avoided going through it. Jesus' attitude toward the Samaritans was surprising (Lk. 9:53–55; Jn. 4).

The Samaritans considered themselves true Israelites, speaking of "our father Jacob" (Jn. 4:12). They called themselves "shomerim," guardians (of the truth). God had bestowed on them creation, and the law through Moses. Moses, whom they never named, was called "the man of God," "the viceroy of the earth." They accepted only the first five books of the Bible. In 330 B.C. a temple was built on Mount Garizim, above Samaria, but in 108 B.C. John Hyrcanus burned it when he destroyed Samaria in reprisal for Samaritan opposition to the rebuilding of Jerusalem.

The Samaritans observed strict monotheism. Moving from their religious mélange in the eighth century, they became very rigid, rejecting anything which had not come from Moses. They observed circumcision, the sabbath, and three feasts: Passover, Pentecost, and Booths. They expected a messiah-judge who would prove them right and put an end to the Jewish schism; this restorer-messiah would be a prophet (cf. Dt. 18:18). Pilate distrusted their ebullience, often reacting to it unjustly. Because of his massacre of Samaritans, he was later suspended from his functions.

A verdant country, Samaria produced grain and fruit. It had many foreign colonies. Herod had repeopled Sebaste-Samaria with six thousand pagan veterans of his army. It had good communications.

Rabbi Simeon ben Eleazar draws from the text of Numbers 15:31: "From this I have proved the falsity of the Samaritans' books, saying that there is no vivifying of the dead: this text means that they will have to give account on the day of judgment.

"Any document signed by a Samaritan witness is invalid except papers of repudiation and of emancipation (of slaves). It is told that an act of repudiation was brought to the Rabbi Gamaliel which had been signed by Samaritans, and he declared it valid."

Chapter 28

The Sanhedrin

The word "sanhedrin" comes from two Greek words: *sun*, meaning group, and *hedra*, seat. It designated a council of notables charged with conducting the political and religious government of Israel.

1. Origin and Composition

The existence of the Sanhedrin is attested from the end of the third century B.C., but it undoubtedly goes back to the Persian period which began with Cyrus in 539. His edict in 538 authorized the return of Jews from exile. About 444, Esdras, a scribe who was working for the material and spiritual restoration of Jerusalem, gathered together a college of priests to classify, protect and interpret the sacred texts. Heads of families also helped him to dissolve the marriages that had been contracted with aliens.

Set up on the model of the councils of Greek cities, the Sanhedrin included priests, elders and notables to assist the high priest, the supreme head of the nation. It saw in itself the image of the seventy individuals who surrounded Moses (Num. 11:16). With the high priest, it had seventy-one members, who met twice a week in the "Hall of Hewn Stones" located on the south side of the court of priests.

Early in the first century before Christ, thanks to Pharisee interest, scribes gained increasing influence. They entered the Sanhedrin, which was thereafter composed of priests, elders and scribes.

Its powers, which had been restricted by Herod, were once again increased by Rome, which did not wish to bother with religious questions.

2. Competence

The Sanhedrin was both a government council and the high court of justice for all Jews, whether living in Palestine or abroad. It meted out justice according to Jewish laws, which were recognized as laws of the empire for all Jews in countries subject to Rome. Its decisions had the force of law and were applied by the Romans, and its competence extended to all religious questions and whatever followed from Jewish law. It did not, however, have the right to impose the death penalty, that right being reserved to the Roman prefect, except in case of a flagrant crime. For example, if a foreigner intruded into the temple, he was immediately put to death. As the Sanhedrin was partly responsible for public order, it had its guard (Jn. 7:32; 18:3).

Two opposing tendencies were represented: the party of the elders and priests, influenced by the Sadducees, and the party influenced by the Pharisees.

In Provinces

There was a tribunal of twenty-three members in each of the principal cities, composed of the leading men of the synagogue, which judged ordinary matters. The role of these tribunals became very important after 70 A.D. when Jerusalem was captured.

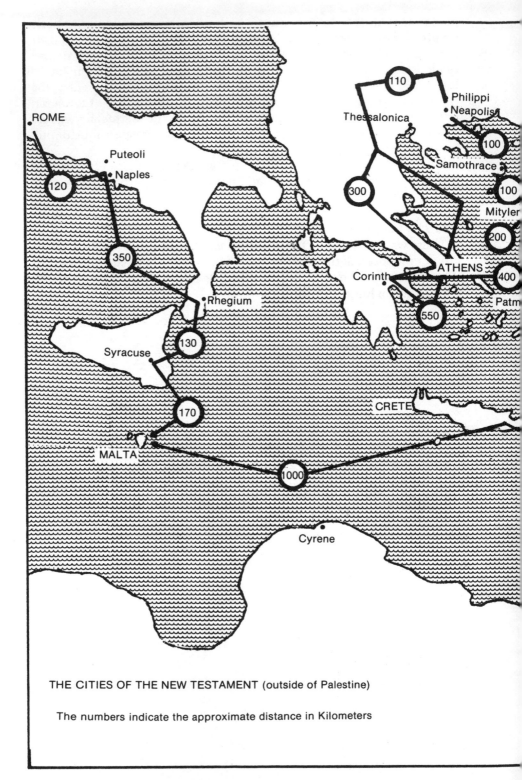

THE CITIES OF THE NEW TESTAMENT (outside of Palestine)

The numbers indicate the approximate distance in Kilometers

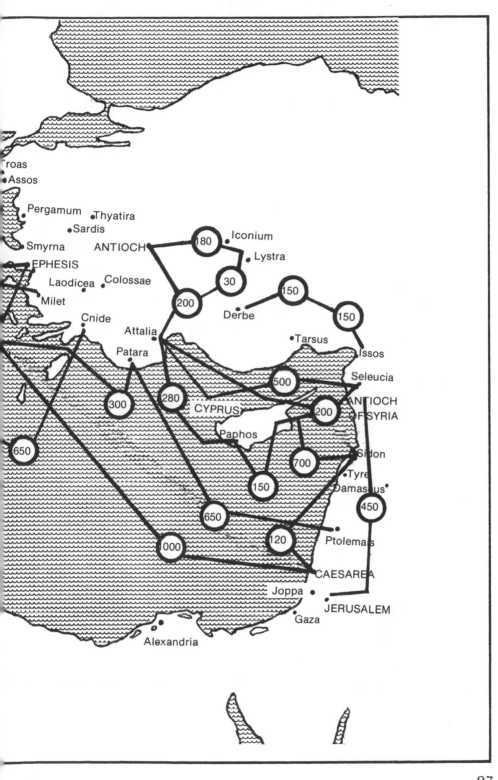

roas
Assos
Pergamum •Thyatira
•Sardis
Smyrna
EPHESIS
Laodicea •Colossae
Milet
Cnide
Attalia
Patara

ANTIOCH
180
Iconium
Lystra
30
200
Derbe
150
150
Tarsus
Issos
Seleucia
500
300
280
CYPRUS
ANTIOCH OF SYRIA
200
650
Paphos
Sidon
700
Tyre
150
Damascus
650
450
000
120
Ptolemais
CAESAREA
Joppa
JERUSALEM
Gaza
Alexandria

Chapter 29

Scribes

The word "scribe" comes from the Latin *scribere*, to write. Scribes were "men of the book," in Hebrew "sopherin," from the verb "saphar," to write. They formed an intellectual aristocracy consisting of jurists, doctors of the law, and specialists in Scripture.

1. Origin

In the beginning, scribes were priests with the duty of explaining and interpreting the law and Scripture. At the same time, there were at the royal court secretaries, translators and, in fact, a whole corps of literary men who could read and write (a very rare accomplishment), who knew the traditions, and who were aware of both domestic and foreign political situations.

After the Babylonian exile, the clergy held political power; the high priest was head of the nation, the royalty having disappeared. There were no more prophets (Ps. 74:9); apparently the last prophet had been Zechariah. Priests occupied themselves with the temple sacrifices. Literate men then gained prestige and uncontested authority, since religious renewal had its roots in observance of the law and its application to the new situation. The scribes were those who taught the law. Consequently, the function of scribes passed from priests to laymen, the scribe Esdras being a good example. After the third century, scribes were nearly all laymen. In the time of Christ, they included laymen (merchants, artisans), a few priests and some Levites.

It was as scribes that the Pharisees entered the Sanhedrin, since their judicial competence suited them for making judgments. Apparently Nicodemus was a scribe (Jn. 3:1; 7:50). Venerated by the people, scribes were of different parties, leaning to either the Sadducees or the Pharisees.

2. Particular Training and Style of Life

Unlike priests, a man did not become a scribe by birth but after a long period of study. The aspirant, as the young student of a master, often pursued his studies with a celebrated teacher in Jerusalem, like Paul at the feet of Gamaliel (Acts 22:3). When he had been well trained, the student became a "non-ordained doctor." He had studied Scripture, civil and religious law (which were the same), and tradition. The "non-ordained doctor" could pass judgment and be a member of a court of justice even in criminal cases.

About the age of forty, the doctor was ordained as a scribe by the imposition of hands. He then sat on the Sanhedrin by right and could "bind and unbind" for all Jews.

Scribes wore a special tunic (Mt. 23:5–6). Men saluted doctors of the law by rising as they passed, except laborers engaged in work. Nonetheless scribes were poor, because they were forbidden to take pay for their services (Mt. 10:8–10). On what, then, did they live?

They lived on charity: on the gratitude of their students, the tithes of the poor, and the alms distributed by the temple. They paid no taxes. Only scribes who were temple officials or priests had fixed revenues. Others carried on some profession to make a living. With eighty students, the great Hillel traveled on foot from Babylon. He was a day laborer and often unemployed. Schammai was a carpenter. Paul was a weaver. Some, however, profited from their legal knowledge (Lk. 20:47). Many developed a taste for the marks of respect shown them (Lk. 20:46) and insisted on being called "rabbi," not master (Lk. 23:7–10).

3. Their Expertise

Considering themselves to have replaced the prophets and to be the successors of the sages, scribes were specialists in religious questions. Usually they were close to the people, unless they had a Sadducee point of view, and they were jealously opposed to oral tradition. Knowing how to read and write Hebrew, the scribes kept to themselves, either for pedagogical reasons or from respect for the reputation of the great families. One part of their knowledge was secret, that involving interpretations of the apocalypses about the messiah, a sort of coded language dealing with the judgment of pagans and liberation by the messiah (Lk. 11:52). This perspective sometimes entailed a strict legalism, a knowledge restricted to the initiated (Mt. 10:27) against which Christ reacted (Mt. 23:23), for "they have raised a hedge around the law" (Mt. 15:6). The oral tradition, often secret, was not mixed in with the written, but served to interpret the written.

The scribes taught in the synagogues. There were two main lines of teaching:

1. that of Hillel, liberal, broad-minded, which sought love of the law;
2. that of Schmmai, emphasizing strict observance.

Though they were close to the Pharisees, the scribes are not to be confused with them. They existed before the Pharisee trend and were not all sympathetic to it. After 70 A.D. the scribes had a prominent role.

Elders

These were heads of families of high social rank, rich and influential, who played a role during and after the exile (Esd. 5:9–16). They were members of the Sanhedrin, often of the conservative, Sadducee tendency. At the time of Christ, their influence had lessened. They were, in particular, the men who knew the traditions and customs and insured social permanence. Joseph of Arimathea was one of them (Mt. 27:57). They were usually landowners and furnished the wood for the temple, a custom which David's family had initiated. They apportioned the taxes exacted by Rome among the citizens and saw to their collection. They therefore worked, often secretly, with the publicans whom they officially despised.

Rabbis

The word "rabbi" means "my master." It was the title of the scribes and then of the learned (Mt. 26:25, 40; Jn. 1:38). There was no institutional form of rabbis until after 70 A.D.

A rabbi said: "I have never grown by humiliating another. I have never received gifts for a judgment, and I have not held jealously to my rights, and I have been generous with my goods."

Chapter 30

The Synagogue

The word "synagogue" comes from two Greek words, *sun* meaning group, and *agoge* meaning meeting. It was a place of prayer and assembly for a Jewish group.

1. Origin

Between 586 and 538 B.C. Israel was in exile. Those who remained in Palestine had no temple, and no sacrifices could be offered, but Jews still gathered to hear a reading of the law and to meditate on it. Places of meeting were originally used only for this purpose, but later the number of synagogues continued to increase. At the time of Christ, there were said to be four hundred and eighty synagogues in Jerusalem, "each with a house of the book to study the law and a schoolroom for study." There were numerous synagogues in the large cities and the Jews of the diaspora had theirs in Jerusalem (Acts 6:9). Often a group, such as a corporation or a village, built its own synagogue. Proselytes and sympathizers could help in this work (Lk. 7:5).

Usually a synagogue was built on a hill or near water (the sea, a lake, a river). It was rectangular, with the portico to the east. At the farther end, a niche contained a small coffer for the rolls of Scripture (the ark). There was a lectern for the reader and commentator. Stone benches along the walls or rugs in the center of the room provided places for the men to sit. Armchairs were provided for important people—scribes and priests (if there were any)—who sat facing the people. Women and children were in a separate place with the slaves, though this was not always true in Palestine. Frescoes or mosaics on biblical scenes adorned the walls. To the side were a study hall for adults and a schoolroom, sometimes merged, and a room for receiving transient guests.

Even when destroyed, the ruins of a synagogue remained a sacred place.

2. Organization

The synagogue was administered by an official chosen from among the elders (Lk. 7:41) and assisted by a council. He structured the liturgy, assigned the readers and invited men he thought qualified to make a commentary (Lk. 4:16–20). He had a trade or cultivated land.

In very large synagogues, the head official was aided by an assistant, the "Harzan," who handed the rolls to the readers, led the prayer and invited any priests present to bless the people. He also gave instructions and was part of a small tribunal as justice of the peace.

3. Worship

Worship was conducted primarily on the sabbath, though people could go every day. The priest's role was simply to bless, not to lead. There had to be at least ten participants. The liturgy depended greatly on people who were able to read. If the reading was in Hebrew, a translator was provided. If there were enough people present who could read, there would be several lectors, and in theory these were selected by rank: priest, Levite, Israelite.

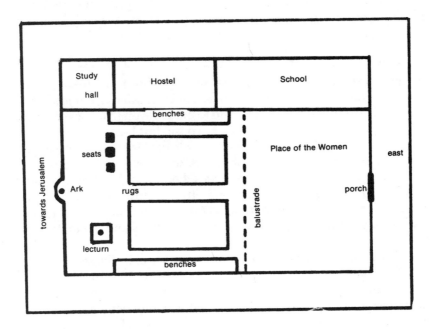

It was a liturgy of the word and included

1. Hymns and prayers (the blessings).
2. Reading of the law.
3. Reading of the prophets.
4. A homily based on the Scripture to apply the text.
5. Recitation of "Hear, O Israel!"
6. Blessing by the priest, if one was present.

In the study hall, discussions were carried on by the scribes.

"The one who reads the law will not read less than three verses. When being interpreted, he will not read more than one verse at a time of the law, but he can read three verses of the prophets, unless the verses are from three different chapters; then he will read them one by one. He can skip from one verse to another in the prophets, but not in the law. How many can be skipped? Not so many that the interpreter has to interrupt."

"We understand that a synagogue's land can be sold only on condition that a synagogue will be rebuilt there."

"No frivolity will be allowed in synagogues. No one may enter to protect himself from the sun, the cold or rain. No one will eat or drink there. No one will stroll there or play there. No one will sleep there. But anyone may read, study or express public mourning there."

There was a plan for reading—for example:
1. If the first day of the twelfth month fell on a sabbath, Exodus 30:11–16 was read. If it fell during the week, the passage was read on the previous sabbath and the continuation on the following sabbath.
2. On the second sabbath, Deuteronomy 25:17–19 was read.
3. On the third sabbath, Numbers 19.
4. On the fourth sabbath, Exodus 12.
5. Then the sequence began again.
6. On feasts, the cycle of readings was interrupted to read:
   On Passover, Leviticus 23.
   On Pentecost, Deuteronomy 16:9.
   On the New Year: Leviticus 23:23ff.
   On the Atonement, Leviticus 16.
   On the Dedication, Numbers 7.

The final blessing: Benediction of the Redemption (primitive version):
"True, firm, solid, durable, right, faithful, loved is this word which is addressed to us for today and forever. The succor of our fathers thou hast been always, buckler and salvation for them, their children after them and for all generations. Rock of Israel, standing for the succor of Israel: according to thy word, deliver Judah and Israel. Our Redeemer, God of Abraham is his name; Holy One of Israel, blessed art thou, Lord, who hast redeemed Israel."

The prayer "Hear, O Israel" was composed of three biblical passages:
    Deuteronomy 6:4–9
    Deuteronomy 11:13–21
    Numbers 15:36–41
recited alternately by the celebrant and the congregation.

Chapter 31

Taxes

The question of taxes is complicated because they varied according to the period and because there was more than one kind.

I. The public treasury at Rome was supplied by:

1. The senate fund, the oldest resource. It was filled by taxes from the senatorial provinces and those in Italy, raised by a questor.
2. Taxes to pay military pensions, created by Augustus from the sale of slaves and inheritances.
3. Taxes levied on imperial provinces.
4. Revenues from the emperor's properties.

II. Direct Roman taxes

Due to Rome by right of conquest. Judea paid six hundred talents. This tax was detested because it symbolized submission to an occupying power. It required a census and a survey; everyone declared what he possessed (cf. Joseph at Bethlehem). The adjusters divided the total sum to be paid to Rome according to:

1. A levy on the land proportionate to the extent of the property, payable in kind (wheat, oil, etc.).
2. A per capita duty, if one did not own land, on personal property.

III. Indirect taxes

1. Customs, which were high in Palestine.
2. Octroi, to enter cities. It was obligatory to declare what was being transported—unless for the temple—on pain of confiscation.

IV. Jewish religious taxes

1. Temple tax, paid annually by everyone, even by Jews living abroad, from the age of twenty (Mt. 17:24). It amounted to two denarii, which equaled two day's work for an agricultural laborer.

3. Tolls, at bridges, gates, cross-roads. Octroi and tolls each represented two to three percent of the value of the merchandise.

N.B. Tithes represented one-tenth of the proceeds of the land but were paid irregularly (Lev. 18:12). They were collected in the summer. A check on their accuracy was made about every three years when the amount due was paid (Dt. 14:28).

2. Tithes, paid in kind or, if in silver, increased by twenty percent. Divided into:

a. Pre-levies or firsts. God owns the land; therefore a tithe of some sort was offered for a first-born child or a first harvest.

b. First tithes (Num. 18:21), on livestock. It was intended for the support of the Levites.

c. Second tithes, paid in silver, for the poor (Dt. 14:26–27).

V. Miscellaneous taxes

For example, Herodian taxes on construction.

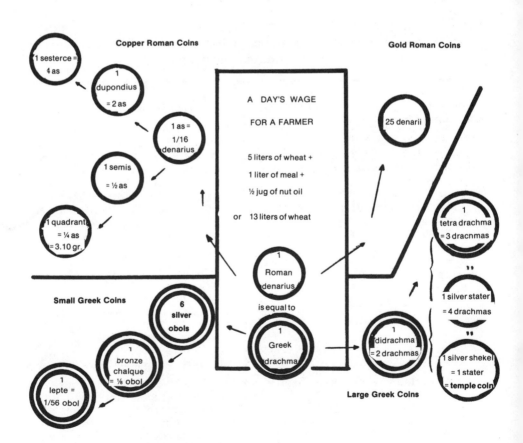

Copper Roman Coins

1 sesterce = 4 as

1 dupondius = 2 as

1 as = 1/16 denarius

1 semis = ½ as

1 quadrant = ¼ as = 3.10 gr.

Small Greek Coins

6 silver obols

1 bronze chalque = ⅛ obol

1 lepte = 1/56 obol

A DAY'S WAGE FOR A FARMER

5 liters of wheat +
1 liter of meal +
½ jug of nut oil

or   13 liters of wheat

1 Roman denarius is equal to

1 Greek drachma

Gold Roman Coins

25 denarii

1 tetra drachma = 3 drachmas

1 silver stater = 4 drachmas

1 silver shekel = 1 stater = temple coin

1 didrachma = 2 drachmas

Large Greek Coins

Results

Roman taxes in Judea amounted to six hundred talents annua...

From Idumea, Judea and Samaria, Archelaus drew five million...mas, or seven hundred talents or twenty-one tons of silver.

Galilee and Perea annually paid two hundred talents or six tons of ...ver.

From his whole kingdom Agrippa I received twelve million drachmas, or fourteen hundred talents, or forty-two tons of silver.

Remarks

The Roman and other governments made a fortune at the expense of the poor.

Indirect taxes were paid by "general tax farmers" who reimbursed themselves generously from those who were poorer. Small taxes were collected by publicans (Matthew).

Rome protected transportation of the temple tax paid in the diaspora.

The Roman denarius was the basic coin, to which the Greek drachma was equivalent. Subdivisions and multiplies:

Roman

1 copper as	equaled	¹⁄₁₆	denarius	1 aureus (gold) equaled 25 denarii
1 dupondous	equaled	2	bronze asses	
1 sesterce	equaled	4	bronze asses	
1 semis	equaled	½	bronze as	
1 quadrant (3.10 gr)	equaled	¼	bronze as	

Greek

1 didrachma	equaled	2 drachmas	1 drac...
1 tetradrachma	equaled	4 drachmas	1 ...
1 silver stater	equaled	4 drachmas	

1 silver shekel (temple coin) of
¼ silver equaled 1 stater
(The last three coins were ...
value)

A day's wages fo... worker:
5 liters of wheat, plus
1 liter of meal, plus
½ amphora of ground nu...

or

13 liters of wheat

Weights which became coins:...
Talent, silver, varied in weigl... tween 27 and 41 kg,; average 34.2... kg. equal to
6,000 denarii
6,000 days' labor
60 silver minas

ome reserved the right to issue currency but gave this right to for small pieces. Herod struck coins.

. Two monetary systems were in effect in principle: that of Rome, hose unit was the denarius with a weight of 3.85 grams (.135 oz.) of silver, and that of Greece, whose unit was the drachma with a weight of 3.50 grams (.125 oz.) of silver. By a convention, the denarius and the drachma were interchangeable. There were also Tyrian coins which were current in the temple.

3. Coins were weighed, and since the weight varied slightly, money changers were able to play with the differences. Equivalences fluctuated because the silver was not pure. The "title," that is, the proportion of pure silver, varied within coins.

4. Prices varied greatly. With a drought they multiplied ten or fifteen times. Speculation was known, particularly in Jerusalem, and devaluation was sometimes as great as twenty percent.

5. Jerusalem was an expensive city, land there being exceptionally costly. In the country, one could buy fifteen figs for an as, but in Jerusalem, not more than three or five.

Chapter 32

The Temple

The temple at Jerusalem was unique for all Jews; only the Samaritans had a concurrent temple on Mount Garizim above Sebaste-Samaria. For a Jew, God dwelt in heaven, that is, he was inaccessible to humans, but, as a witness to his covenant with his people, God made his glory rest in the temple. There was one faith, one God, one temple. As the sign of God's real presence with his people, the temple was the center of Judaism. The most sacred part was divided in two by a heavy veil (Mt. 27:51–52). The forecourt, the larger, was the "Holy." The second, the "Holy of Holies," was completely empty, for no man could make an image of God, and the high priest went into it only once a year, on the Day of Atonement. A tradition places the temple on Mount Moreh, where Abraham offered Isaac. The people were greatly attached to the temple, which received many gifts (Lk. 21:5).

The first temple, built by Solomon in 931 B.C., was destroyed in 587. The second temple was built after the exile, between 520 and 516, but it was profaned by Antiochus IV in 165 B.C., reconsecrated in 164, and unharmed by Pompey in 63.

For political reasons, to gain the good will of the Jews, Herod the Great started to rebuild the temple in 20–19. It was opened in 10–9 and finished in 64 A.D. The Romans, under Titus, burned it in 70 A.D.

Description of Herod's Temple

Herod had kept the plan of Solomon's temple, situated on an east-west axis. He considerably embellished it and had it start from an esplanade whose terraces were raised to a level of one hundred to one hundred and sixty-five feet above the ground. The surface of the whole covered a rectangle about sixteen hundred feet by one thousand feet, surrounded by a wall with towers at the corners and the gates. The northwest corner coincided with the military citadel Antonia, built by Herod and used as quarters for the Roman garrison. The southeast tower from a height of five hundred feet dominated the Cedron valley which separated the temple from the Mount of Olives. Every morning a sentinel there greeted the new day.

Entry from the city was by a bridge which crossed the Tyropoeon ravine. This led to a terrace with four gates, and thence onto the esplanade, an immense courtyard, seven hundred and fifty feet wide, which surrounded the sanctuary. Paved with flagstones and mosaics, this esplanade was encircled by porches. The largest was the royal porch, a veritable basilica, with three naves separated by four rows of forty-two columns ninety feet in height. The central span was forty feet wide. The ceiling was sculptured cedar. On the east, Solomon's porch had 268 columns, thirty-five feet high. The other porches had a width of fifty feet. There were rooms, storehouses and halls in the porches. Merchants set up at the gates and sometimes invaded the porches and esplanades; this esplanade was the Court of Pagans.

To the north, a low wall about three feet high formed the barrier which uncircumcised pagans could not pass under pain of immediate death, as they were warned by posters in several languages. On three sides, nine flights of steps rose an average of ten feet, from five to fourteen steps, the north being elevated. At this point the second court led into the Court of

> "Let no foreigner go inside the barrier and into sacred precincts. Whoever will be caught will be liable to immediate death."

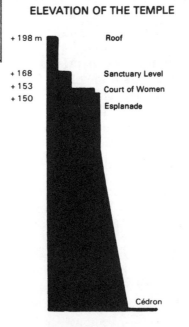

ELEVATION OF THE TEMPLE

+ 198 m — Roof

+ 168 — Sanctuary Level
+ 153 — Court of Women
+ 150 — Esplanade

Cédron

Women, 220 feet square. At each corner was a small room, one for wood, one for oil and water, one each for Nazarenes (who had made a vow) and lepers coming to be examined. There were nine gates, the decorated "beautiful gate" being at the east. Many beggars took their places there, alongside the collection boxes (Lk. 21:1).

From the west, entry was by the solemn Nicanor gate, very heavy and closed at night, to reach the third court, the Court of Men, which a boy could enter at the age of twelve. It is not known whether there was a separate Court of Priests, or whether laymen kept to the area around the Court of Priests, a strip about 17 to 20 feet wide except on the west, not separated from the court. In the center was the altar of sacrifice, a block of stone 47 by 47 by 14 feet, the corners of which were shaped like horns. Fire burned. A ramp allowed animals to be led in, and a drain carried off the blood and the water which an underground canal fed into the Cedron gardens for an annual rental. To the north of the altar there were four rows of six sealed rings for attaching the animals. Further to the north, on eight pillars, cedar beams held the quarters of meat, the beams being connected with the "abbatoir house." To the west of the altar there was a large basin of water fed by an aqueduct. There were marble tables on which to put instruments and to cut up the victims.

The temple, built by priests, stood one hundred feet high at the front. The sanctuary level was thirty-seven feet above the Court of the Priests. The surface of the face, three thousand square feet, was overlaid with gold, although the gold eagle which Herod had placed on it had been torn away. At the top of the steps was a vestibule eighteen feet long, the

From remotest times, the seven-branched candlestick had commemorated the seven planets in the Babylonian sky, the seven levels of the Mesopotamian ziggurat, or prayer tower, and later the seven heavens above which God was enthroned and the seven days of creation.

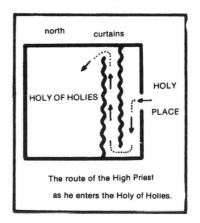

The route of the High Priest as he enters the Holy of Holies.

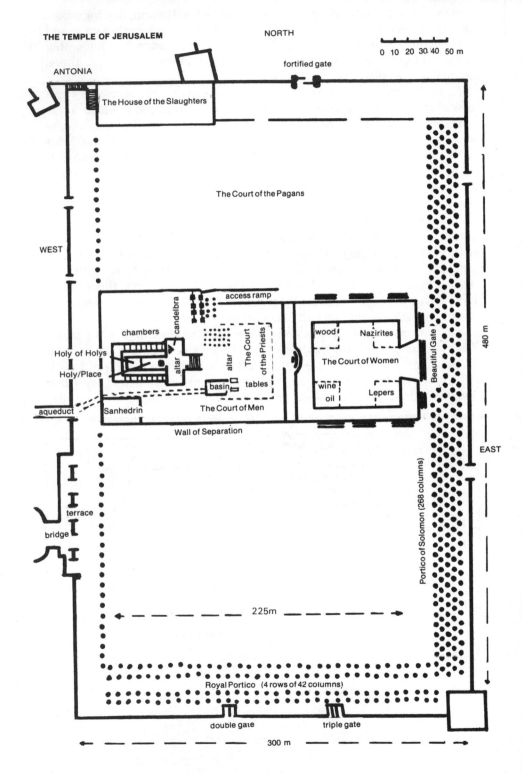

THE TEMPLE OF JERUSALEM

NORTH

0 10 20 30 40 50 m

ANTONIA

fortified gate

The House of the Slaughters

The Court of the Pagans

WEST

access ramp

candelbra

chambers

Holy of Holys

Holy/Place

Holy of Holys

altar

The Court of the Priests

altar

wood   Nazirites

The Court of Women

480 m

Beautiful Gate

basin   tables

aqueduct   Sanhedrin

wine
oil   Lepers

The Court of Men

EAST

Wall of Separation

terrace

Portico of Solomon (268 columns)

bridge

225m

Royal Portico (4 rows of 42 columns)

double gate   triple gate

300 m

"ulam." A door which was closed at night and protected by a curtain during the day led into the "Holy," the "Hekal." Above the door was a golden vine, the symbol of Israel (cf. Jn. 15).

The "Holy" was a rectangle sixty-five by thirty-three feet panelled with precious woods inlaid with gold. In it reposed the golden seven-branched candlestick, seven feet in height, the table for the loaves of proposition inlaid with gold, and the altar of perfumes, also gold inlaid and used twice daily.

At the far end was the "Holy of Holies," the "Debir," the most holy place. It was separated from the Holy by two curtains so that neither a glance nor light could penetrate it. The high priest went in once a year to place a smoking censer on a bare stone. The walls were inlaid with gold. After 586 B.C. the ark of the covenant was no longer there.

Details: There was a space above the temple whose use is not known. A balustrade three feet high surrounded the whole, broken with gilded points to discourage birds from resting there. The stone of the temple was very white. The temple employed twenty thousand people. It retained the old currency struck during independence (165–63 B.C.), the silver shekel which was equivalent to four denarii. Grouped in corporations, the employees were guaranteed against unemployment but were paid less than others. In 70 A.D. the Romans took two thousand talents of gold; the price of gold dropped by half in Syria.

The Idea of a Unique Temple

It is certain that the establishment of a single sanctuary began with Solomon's policy. Deuteronomy describes the beginning of its long history. This book was rediscovered—hence it had previously existed—under King Josiah in 622 B.C. It is thought that this book was written after the failure of King Hezekiah (707–687) to effect the religious reforms he had undertaken. He had sought to centralize worship in Jerusalem; therefore, Solomon's centralization had not been fully successful.

> "He removed the high places and broke down the pillars and cut down the Asherah. He broke in pieces the brazen serpent that Moses had made . . . for the people of Israel had burned incense to it." (2 Kgs. 18:4)

Shortly before Hezekiah, priests and Levites had arrived in Jerusalem fleeing from Samaria which had been occupied by the Assyrians in 722 B.C. These refugees brought with them two traditions from the north which had been strongly held around the temple at Shechem.

Accepting the traditions brought from the north as well as all the reforming efforts of Hezekiah, the Book of Deuteronomy reported of the temple at Jerusalem everything which had been said of the principal sanctuaries before Solomon and which had remained alive, especially in the north.

"You shall surely destroy all the places where the nations whom you shall dispossess served their gods upon the high mountains, upon the hills and under every green tree; you shall tear down their altars and dash to pieces their pillars, you shall burn their Asherim. . . . You shall not do so to the Lord your God. But you shall seek the place which the Lord your God will choose out of all your tribes and make his habitation there" (Dt. 12:2–5).

Actually this passage, which was applied to Jerusalem, could be originally understood perhaps for the temple at Shechem, which Joshua built on Mount Ebal (Jos. 8:30–35).

Another great center in the middle of Palestine, Shiloh, had been destroyed by the Philistines and yet God had there "made his name dwell" (Jer. 7:12).

After the exile, the rebuilding of the temple at Jerusalem crystallized at a single site, the place where "Yahweh made his name dwell."

Summing up, three factors made the single temple at Jerusalem practicable:

1. Solomon's political centralization;
2. the destruction of the kingdom of the North by the Assyrians;
3. the rebuilding of the temple at Jerusalem after the exile.

Other Temples

While the disappearance of other sanctuaries made Jerusalem's pre-eminence possible, we know of other attempts to revive sanctuaries:

1. The Samaritans' temple built under Alexander the Great on Mount Garizim and destroyed by the high priest John Hyrcanus.

2. According to several papyrii, there was a temple at Elephantine which served a small Jewish community occupying a military post in Pharaoh's service. This temple was destroyed by the Persian invasion of Egypt in 480. It engaged in a curious cult about which very little is known.

3. At the time of the disturbances in 170 B.C., the high priest Onias took his family to Egypt, where there was already a large Jewish colony. In the southern part of the Nile delta, at Leontopolis, he established a temple built according to the one at Jerusalem which, apparently, was more or less tolerated. The Romans destroyed it in 53 A.D. It was from Leontopolis, incidentally, that Herod brought back a priest whom he made high priest.

Chapter 33

Zealots

The word "zealot" comes from the Greek and means one who is "zealous for" the law, an ardent defender of the law.

This group grew from two very different origins. On the one hand, there had long been companies of brigands in Galilee who were solidly entrenched in the mountains. These outlaws even controlled the pilgrimage roads to the very borders of Jerusalem. As governor of Galilee, Herod made merciless war on them in 47 B.C. and exterminated them, thus insuring the safety of the roads. Thence the name "bandits" or "brigands," which was how the local powers regarded the Zealots.

On the other hand, Galilee was the site of ongoing nationalist insurrection which was extremist and very rigid in religious matters. This turmoil was sparked by the increase in large estates, often possessed by foreigners, and by the settling of Greek people in the cities built or restored by Herod.

Living like outlaws, the rebels organized in 47 B.C. under the command of Ezachias of Gamala, against the power of Herod over Galilee. Herod captured and killed Ezachias and dispersed his followers. The Sanhedrin, revolted by the violence of this punitive expedition and partly approving the rebels' religious motives, favored condemning Herod, who was never to forgive them. After 31 B.C. Herod had forty-five members of the Sanhedrin killed because of their partiality for the old priestly family of the Hasmoneans.

When Herod the Great died in 4 B.C. and a new census was undertaken in Judea to determine taxes between 4 B.C. and 6 A.D. by Quirinus, the legate of Syria, Judas the Galilean, son of Ezachias (cf. Acts 5:37) revolted. He took the arsenal at Sepphoris and caused disturbances in Galilee. Some people took him for the Messiah. The Romans helped Antipas restore calm and he repaired the damage to Sepphoris.

The agitation was never to be completely put down, and little by little war became inevitable. The nationalist sentiment grew sharper. Although the name "Zealot" appeared in 66, the movement goes back much further. The apostle Simon the Zealot, or Canaanean (from the Aramaic "zealous"), was one of them (Mt. 10:4), but Jesus rejected the extremist ideology of the Zealots (Mt. 19:16). In November 66, a leading Zealot, John, took possession of Jerusalem, and the rebellion became open war. They burned the archives, particularly the list of debts.

The Sicara

The word comes from the Latin *sica*, meaning dagger; sicarius came to mean assassin. The dagger men operated against Rome at times of feasts and big gatherings (e.g., Barabbas; cf Lk. 23:10). They were very active under the procurator Felix (52–60) and engaged in the kidnaping of hostages under the venal Albinus (62–64) to obtain the release of political prisoners. They had sympathizers among the Jews. The Jewish historian Flavius Josephus charges them with the assassination of the old high priest Jonathan on behalf of the procurator.

The following is a comment by the Jewish historian Flavius Josephus in the first century A.D. in regard to the Zealots, to whom he was not sympathetic.

"Quirinus, a Roman senator, a man of great merit, had achieved many degrees of honors. He was elevated to the dignity of consul. Augustus made him governor of Syria with orders to take a new census of all properties of individuals. With him was sent Coponius, who commanded a corps of cavalry, to govern Judea. However, as this province had been attached to Syria, it was not he, but rather Quirinus who made the census during which he seized all the silver which had belonged to Archelaus.

"At first the Jews could not support this new census. The high priest Eleazar-ben-Beothos persuaded them not to resist. But some time afterward, a certain person named Judas from the city of Gamala in Gaulanitis, aided by a Pharisee named Zadok, aroused the people to an uprising, saying that this new census proved on its face that it was desired to reduce them to slavery. To exhort them to keep their freedom, he showed them that if they succeeded they could then have the benefit of repose and all their properties with glory but they ought not to count on the assistance of God if they did nothing of what lay in their power. The people responded to this speech; they revolted. It is impossible to think of the disturbance which these two men aroused on every side. They were nothing but murderers and robbers. Friends and enemies were pillaged indiscriminately on the pretext of defending freedom. The rage of these rebels went so far as to attack cities at a time when famine had occurred and even to the shedding of the blood of those of their own country. And we even saw the fire reach the temple of God.

"The sect of Judas agreed in all things with the Pharisees except on this one point: it is God alone who is to be recognized as Lord and King. They so love freedom that they endure all sufferings, for themselves and for theirs, rather than give to a man the title of lord and master."

Flavius Josephus, Jewish Antiquities, 18, 1–2

Judas the apostle might have been part of this group. (Some liken the name Iscariot to Sicara, but the etymology is dubious.) He may have betrayed Christ because he was disillusioned on seeing Jesus refuse to be the Zealot Messiah when he defended the payment of taxes (Mt. 22:15–22) which the Zealots refused to do.

The Translator
Sister Alice Alexander, a member of the Ursuline Order, was,
until her retirement, librarian at the College of New Rochelle.
Before entering the Order, she had been in the service of the
Department of State, both in Washington, in the Translating
Division, and in several foreign posts.